THE INSIDE GUIDE TO LIVERPOOL

TrinityMirror Media

EDITOR:
Vicky Andrews

DESIGN:
Zoe Bevan, Lisa Critchley, Colin Harrison

CONTRIBUTORS:
Paul Baker, David Charters, James Cleary, Dawn Collison, Keith Curtis, Laura Davis, John Dempsey, Peter Elson, Peter Grant, Jane Haase, Sarah Hooley, Alan Jewell, Emma Johnson, Catherine Jones, Marc Jones, Sue Kelbrick, Tony Martin, Katie McLoughlin, Ken Pye, Joe Riley, Michelle Rushton, Stephen Shakeshaft, Paddy Shennan, Emma Thompson, Karen Timms, Luke Traynor, Jade Wright, Richie Wright

IMAGES:
All images from the Liverpool Daily Post & Echo archives unless otherwise stated.

SPECIAL THANKS TO
Dave Humphreys
(www.flickr.com/photos/dangerous_disco)
Sakura (rockphotographer.net)

PUBLISHED BY
Trinity Mirror Media
PO Box 48, Old Hall Street, Liverpool L69 3EB

PRINTED BY
Pensord Magazine and Periodicals
Tram Road, Pontllanfraith, Blackwood NP12 2YA
www.pensord.co.uk

ISBN
9781906802462

CONTENTS

LIVERPOOL
ECHO

AS editor of the ECHO, let me welcome you to the new Liverpool.

A city where ancient meets modern in a thrilling blend of tradition and contemporary excitement. A city reborn and riding high on the back of its year as European Capital of Culture.

This guide is here to make sure you get the best from this extraordinary place. The ECHO has been at the heart of Liverpool life for 30 years. Our team of writers have encyclopaedic knowledge of the best entertainment, the cultural gems, the superb restaurants, the smartest bars, the fantastic new shops.

If you are visiting, let my team take you through the city's remarkable past and into its stunning present.

And if you live here then we'll help you marvel at the astounding transformation that's taken place around you.

Whoever you are, whatever you crave, Liverpool has it. Our Capital of Culture slogan called it 'A World in One City'.

It's a sentiment I am proud to 'Echo'.

Alistair Machray

VICKY ANDREWS

Book Editor by day and DJ by night, Vicky is often found bleary-eyed, waxing lyrical about the latest bands and clubs. A broadcast and newspaper journalist for fifteen years, she has her finger on the city's pulse.

CATHERINE JONES

Five star arts editor of the Liverpool ECHO. She covered the city's status as European Capital of Culture. Catherine once described herself as 'notoriously cynical'. A born critic.

PETER ELSON

National Maritime Writer of the Year in 2010. That says it all about one of the most-respected feature writers in the Merseyside area, reporting on land and sea and always making editorial waves.

JADE WRIGHT

If pop's the question, Jade can answer it. An award-winning music writer who has the eyes and ears of many of today's stars. She has a bulging contact book and knows what's hot and what's not.

PETER GRANT

Journalist, broadcaster and author and still he can't get a proper job. Peter has been in newspapers for 30 years and has a Liverpool ECHO blog called Granty's Scouse Pie. An expert on the Beatles and anything Scouse – know worra mean, like, la.

EMMA JOHNSON

A sparkling writer who knows everything there is to know about restaurants, bars, lifestyle and fashion. Her weekly Clubbing column bounces off the page of the ECHO every Friday and is a must read for youngsters in the city.

ALAN JEWELL

You can call him Al – a diamond in the squad of sports writers. Alan can turn his hand to anything sporting, as his informed views, comments and analysis always show. A premiership player in the critics' league.

PADDY SHENNAN

While, for some, pubs may be mainly about fruit machines and mass-produced lager, Paddy takes his pub-going experience more seriously – he's even won awards. We'll drink to that.

08

WELCOME to LIVERPOOL

NEW Liverpool is associated with passion, spirit, creativity and big investment. Whether you have been here five minutes, five years or 50 years, there is something new to discover.

Liverpool has certainly come of age. The Liverpool ONE and Met Quarter developments have helped push Liverpool into the top five in the national retail league. The ECHO Arena Liverpool, cruise liner terminal and the Pier Head canal link have added new life to the waterfront, already a UNESCO World Heritage Site.

New pedestrian connections between the docks and the city now enhance this experience. The commercial sector is also expanding with new office space popping up, seemingly every day.

These additions have been built on Liverpool's already impressive architectural heritage – the Three Graces, St George's Hall, our two cathedrals and the largest number of listed buildings outside London.

Easy to reach and pretty effortless to explore, for every visitor to Liverpool there is a new convert to its charms, whether it's the award-winning restaurants, the cutting-edge boutiques, the world-famous galleries and museums or the beauty of our parks and open spaces. If you get lost, just ask one of the natives.

It's people that make a city and the unique experience of Liverpool life has made it a cool place to be.

So, take the time to look up and around you, and appreciate the cultural wealth that surrounds you.

And then tell others about it.

SITE for GOOD EYES

■ The magnificent St George's Hall facade stands out in all its glory against a blue sky backdrop. Above, Mann Island takes on a new shape

LIVERPOOL is in great company. The pyramids – you can't say pharaoh than that. Oh, and the Great Wall of China.

We are cultural neighbours. Liverpool is a UNESCO World Heritage Site – now that's global.

But this is pure Liverpool heritage. The World Heritage status means that we more than met the criteria in having 'a monument; group of buildings or some structure, which is of outstanding universal value to the international community.'

The award was made on the basis that the Site is 'the supreme example of a commercial port at a time of Britain's greatest global influence'. We got it.

Our award-winning area stretches along the waterfront from Albert Dock, through the Pier Head and up to Stanley Dock, and on through the historic commercial districts and the fascinating RopeWalks area to the cultural quarter which is dominated by St George's Hall.

Liverpool – Maritime Mercantile City World Heritage Site – is one of 850 cultural and natural World Heritage 'sites'. As well as putting us alongside The Great Wall of China and the Pyramids of Giza, we are up there with the cities of Edinburgh and Bath.

Liverpool's historic significance centres on its involvement in the growth of world trade, mercantile culture, the trans-Atlantic slave trade and mass European emigration.

The World Heritage Site also includes a short stretch of the Leeds and Liverpool Canal, which, with the opening of the new canal link in 2009, now provides access by barge across the Pier Head and right up to the Albert Dock, via the refurbished Stanley Locks and the historic dock system.

A site to be seen.

The Walker Art Gallery

Inside St George's Hall

LIVERPOOL'S BIGGEST STAR

KING John knew that the river WAS Liverpool even back in 1208. He gave the city a charter because of it.

The river lies at the foot of the city like a loyal age-old dog. Rarely silent, its drowsy, murmuring, flickering waves twitch in a gently dreaming wind. Liverpool Bay breathes softly as the widening tide stirs and stretches out to sea.

A sudden twitch, and the pulse quickens as wind wakes and breaks the swell. Disturbed, the river surges, shakes and growls as it rises up the dock walls. It presses against the side of the city, restlessly pounding over the broken rocks and grinding chains.

Urging attention it rages, quietly first, then louder, clamouring in a mounting gale, scaling the walls it sprawls into the lap of the land. It snaps at the heels of strange ships, harries the hulls of colossal containers and follows the foam from the ferry boats.

It wrestles the sails and nuzzles the nobbies and bobbing buoys. It runs out with the tide for mile after mile after mile. But it will always return, wearying as the moon wanes.

Waiting at the foot of the city. People sittin' at the dock of the Bay – did Otis Redding come here?

The Mersey is the city's lifeblood. Generations made their living by it – millions sailed on it and, to this day, Liverpudlians and visitors love it. Liverpool's biggest tourist attraction – and it's free . . . always has been and always will be.

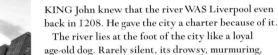

San Carlo, Castle Street

COME DINE with ME

OVER the last decade the city has undergone a food revolution.

The restaurant scene is now bustling with establishments offering cuisine from the four corners of the gastronomic globe.

Old favourites like The Quarter and The Everyman Bistro have been joined by new players like the London Carriage Works, Simply Heathcotes and San Carlo.

We have delis and diners, Spanish restaurants and sushi bars, Greek tavernas and gastro pubs. We even have one of the highest restaurants in the country in the shape of Panoramic, 34 floors above street level. In June 2010, celebrity chef Jamie Oliver will bring his own brand of Italian cooking to the city with his new restaurant in Liverpool ONE – the venue will be the first Jamie's Italian to open in the North West. But good food does not stop at the city limits.

From the centre of Church Street to the Cheshire and Lancashire borders there are great dishes to be devoured. And thanks to Wirral restaurateur Marc Wilkinson of Fraiche, Merseyside finally has its very first Michelin star. Never has dining out been more exciting.

Beyonce at the
ECHO Arena Liverpool

BIGGER than the BEATLES

JOHN, Paul, George and Ringo might have been four lads who shook the world – but if the Beatles were the only artists to have emerged from Liverpool, then the city would never have been named 'the World City of Pop' by the Guinness Book of Records in 2001 or named 'the UK's Most Musical City' by the Arts Council in 2008.

Liverpool is proud of its musical heritage, but we also have festivals like Creamfields, Liverpool Music Week and Sound City.

The 11,000-capacity ECHO Arena has hosted the likes of Lady Gaga, Kings of Leon, Beyonce, Bob Dylan and the 2008 MTV Europe Music Awards. No longer do we miss out to that city at the other end of the M62 – even Oasis kicked off their last homecoming tour in Liverpool. Mathew Street today seems worlds away from the dingy sidestreet of legend, and mixed in with the salty breeze from the Atlantic is an unmistakable sense of optimism.

Liverpool is already a UNESCO World Heritage City and in spring 2010 the city officially handed in its bid to join an exclusive club of just four other UNESCO world cities of music.

The city has a phenomenal pool of talent and it's exciting that now, more than ever, it has the gigs, the studios, the promoters and the festivals to nurture new ideas and artists who will carry on Liverpool's diverse musical traditions.

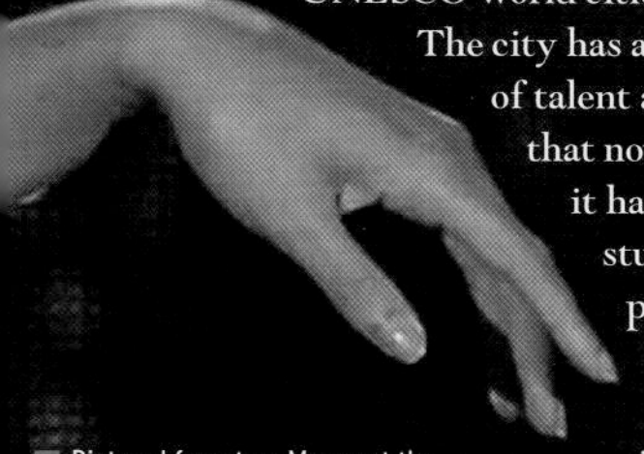

■ Pictured from top; Macca at the MTV Awards, Creamfields, Brouhaha Carnival, Vasily Petrenko at The Philharmonic Hall, The Rascals (photo by Sakura)

THE FUTURE is BRIGHT

Peel Holdings' vision for Liverpool Waters

ALONG with popular music, architecture is one of the key aspects of Liverpool's cultural status.

Liverpool's urgency to regenerate is spelled out across the rising skyline, from the new museum development at Mann Island, to the towering Contemporary Urban Centre in the Baltic Triangle. When the new Lime Street Gateway is completed in 2010, this entrance to the city – with its stunning aspect of St George's Hall – will provide an awe-inspiring welcome.

The Baltic Creative scheme, boosted by a £5.2m investment plan, will see four buildings off Jamaica Street refurbished to house creative and digital businesses, breathing new life into the area around the CUC and New Picket.

The Pier Head Buildings made bold statements in their day and new buildings taking shape at Mann Island are doing the same thing. The development includes apartments, cafes, restaurants and shops, as well as spaces earmarked for the new Merseytravel headquarters and Open Eye Gallery.

The largest newly-built national museum in the UK for over a hundred years will demonstrate Liverpool's unique contribution to the world.

With the Titanic Centenary on the horizon in 2012, Liverpool will tell the real people's story, the glamour, tragedy and mystery behind the White Star Line's 'unsinkable' ocean liner. Liverpool can lay a stronger claim to the Titanic than New York, Belfast or Southampton – the potential is, well, titanic. No iceberg analogies allowed.

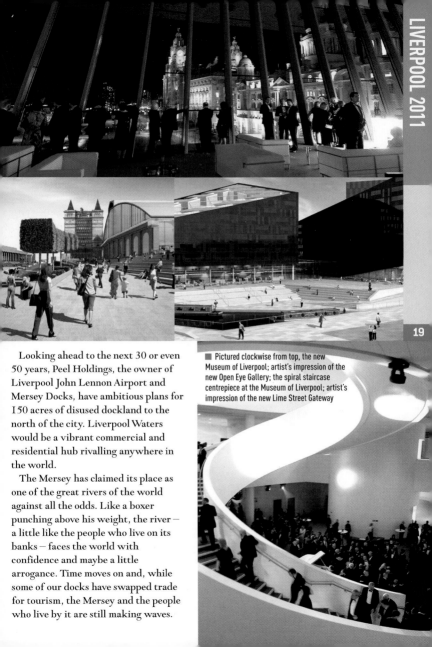

Looking ahead to the next 30 or even 50 years, Peel Holdings, the owner of Liverpool John Lennon Airport and Mersey Docks, have ambitious plans for 150 acres of disused dockland to the north of the city. Liverpool Waters would be a vibrant commercial and residential hub rivalling anywhere in the world.

The Mersey has claimed its place as one of the great rivers of the world against all the odds. Like a boxer punching above his weight, the river – a little like the people who live on its banks – faces the world with confidence and maybe a little arrogance. Time moves on and, while some of our docks have swapped trade for tourism, the Mersey and the people who live by it are still making waves.

■ Pictured clockwise from top, the new Museum of Liverpool; artist's impression of the new Open Eye Gallery; the spiral staircase centrepiece at the Museum of Liverpool; artist's impression of the new Lime Street Gateway

Waiting to take you away...

There are an abundance of fascinating things to see and do in Liverpool, many of which may be right under the noses of even the most knowledgeable residents. Here are some of the tours available in the city, so why not discover something new in Liverpool?

CULTURE VULTURE

City Sightseeing Tours
0151 203 3920

www.city-sightseeing.com

Seeing the city in style couldn't be easier, with this open-top bus tour of Liverpool's most famous landmarks – hop on and off at 12 stops, including the historic waterfront, cathedrals, museums, galleries and Chinatown. The tour departs every 30 minutes, starting at Canada Boulevard at the famous Liver Buildings, and lasts one hour.

FAB FOUR

Magical Mystery Tour

www.cavernclub.org

The Magical Mystery Tour takes you on a journey through the Beatles' lives, even stopping at their childhood homes and schools and the places that inspired them to create some of their best music. There is a running commentary from a guide to ensure that you know what exactly you are witnessing.

GHOSTLY ENCOUNTERS
Shiverpool Ghost Tours
0151 709 2030
www.shiverpool.co.uk
Forty thousand people have been shaken by Shiverpool – some haven't made it back to tell the tale – will you? Shiverpool Ghost Tours offer a walking tour around some of the oldest buildings and their spooky inhabitants. Discover Liverpool's most famous ghosts on the Hope Street Shivers tour, starting at The Philharmonic Pub and ending at the Anglican Cathedral. Horror at St George's Hall is an eerie journey through the cells and courtroom – guaranteed to send shivers down your spine. Tours run all year and can take up to 40 people – but don't be fooled into thinking there's safety in numbers – watch out for the 'others' lurking around hidden corners . . .

MINE'S A PINT
The Cains Brewery Tour
0151 709 8734
www.cains.co.uk
If you'd rather spend an afternoon in the pub than go on a tourist trail then the obvious answer is to head to Cains Brewery. A fascinating insight into Merseyside's rich brewing heritage and includes two complimentary pints of Cains' award-winning ales. Tours take place Monday through to Friday and begin at 6.30pm; Saturday and Sunday at 1pm. Tours must be pre-booked. Unfortunately not suitable for the less agile due to a lot of Victorian stairs

GERRY CROSS THE MERSEY
River Explorer Cruises
0151 639 0609
www.merseyferries.co.uk
The best way to see Liverpool's stunning waterfront. This cruise across the Mersey lasts 50 minutes and departs from the Pier Head on the hour. Featuring commentary about the city's history and architecture and, of course, that famous song. All together now, "Life, goes on day after day . . ."

WALK THIS WAY
Red Jack Tours
www.redjacktours.com
A three-and-a-half mile walking tour of the city, taking in the historic waterfront, city centre, Mathew Street and the cathedrals, with an insightful commentary on the history, culture and humour of the city. Lasting about 2 hours, the tour starts on Strand Street near the entrance to the Albert Dock, where participants will be greeted by Alan with his red and white umbrella. Tours take place at 2pm on Saturdays and Sundays (where walkers can turn up 'on spec') and run from Easter to October. 10am Saturday tours can be pre-booked through the website, for a minimum of five people

HEAD FOR HEIGHTS
Radio City Tower Tour
0151 472 6800
www.radiocity.co.uk
The futuristic 400ft Radio City Tower – home to Radio City 96.7 – offers stunning 360 degree views of the Liverpool skyline. Visitors can take a full tour of St John's Beacon and the radio studios. Tours are held hourly, Monday – Friday at 3pm, 4pm, 5pm and 6pm. The viewing gallery is open Saturday and Sunday from 10am till late.

QUACKY RACES
The Yellow Duckmarine
0151 708 7799
www.theyellowduckmarine.co.uk
Is it a boat? Is it a bus? No – it's a duck! Any the wiser? Probably not! What it really is, is one of two WW II DUKW amphibious landing craft that The Yellow Duckmarine company has rebuilt, updated and turned into a 30-seat sightseeing vehicle. These 1-hour sightseeing tours depart from the Albert Dock. The company also runs Yellow Boat Cruises around the south docks. You'd be quackers to miss it

TICKET to RIDE

WORKS of public art are everywhere, but often we barely notice them. Emma Lawrence, Merseytravel's public arts officer, gives us a guide to some of the art that Merseytravel has commissioned.

PIER HEAD FERRY TERMINAL

The John Newton Sculpture or 'Amazing Grace' was created by the artist Stephen Broadbent. It's a huge piece, gracing the wall inside the Pier Head Ferry Terminal building and is dedicated to the memory of the former Tide Surveyor of Liverpool, John Newton. Newton campaigned to abolish slavery and also penned the words to the hymn Amazing Grace.

BOOTLE ORIEL ROAD

Giant steel sculpture 'Past, Present and Future' by local artist Stephen Hitchin, stands over eight metres tall. It reflects and celebrates the history and growth of Bootle and its people.

BIRKENHEAD PARK STATION

Time and Place is made up of three sculptures, standing over five metres tall, each holding three semi-circles depicting places from across Wirral and Merseyside. Each time you view these sculptures your eyes pick out something new; be it St John's Beacon or La Princesse, the mechanical spider.

LIVERPOOL SOUTH PARKWAY

The Grand National Mural stretches high up the wall against the station's elevator shaft. Artist Janet Shearer has used the technique Trompe L'oeil to depict every Grand National winner of the previous two decades tackling Aintree's infamous Canal Turn.

LIME STREET

Two famous faces of Liverpool welcome you here – comedian Ken Dodd, alongside the Liverpool MP and social reformer Bessie Braddock. These life-size bronze statues are full of detail and character, with Ken brandishing his famous tickle-stick and Bessie holding an egg marked with the British Lion stamp of quality, which was her own brainchild.

Merseyrail

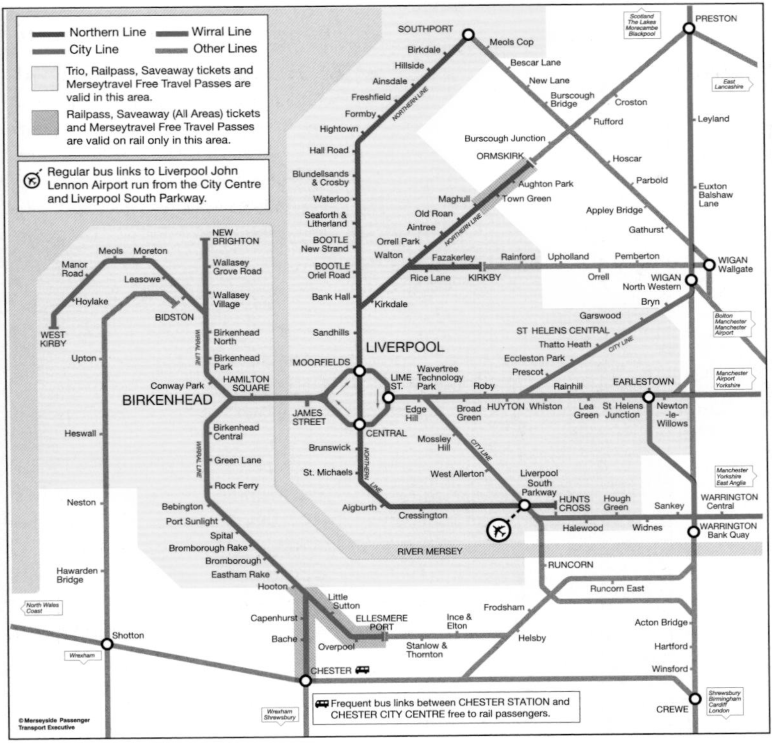
Northern Line
Wirral Line
City Line
Other Lines
Trio, Railpass, Saveaway tickets and Merseytravel Free Travel Passes are valid in this area.
Railpass, Saveaway (All Areas) tickets and Merseytravel Free Travel Passes are valid on rail only in this area.
Regular bus links to Liverpool John Lennon Airport run from the City Centre and Liverpool South Parkway.
SOUTHPORT
Meols Cop
Birkdale
Hillside
Ainsdale
Freshfield
Formby
Hightown
Hall Road
Blundellsands & Crosby
Waterloo
Seaforth & Litherland
BOOTLE New Strand
BOOTLE Oriel Road
Bank Hall
Sandhills
MOORFIELDS
LIVERPOOL
LIME ST.
JAMES STREET
CENTRAL
Brunswick
St. Michaels
Aigburth
Cressington
NORTHERN LINE
Bescar Lane
New Lane
Burscough Bridge
Croston
Rufford
Burscough Junction
ORMSKIRK
Hoscar
Parbold
Aughton Park
Town Green
Maghull
Old Roan
Aintree
Orrell Park
Walton
Kirkdale
Fazakerley
Rice Lane
KIRKBY
Rainford
Upholland
Orrell
Pemberton
Appley Bridge
Gathurst
PRESTON
Leyland
Euxton Balshaw Lane
WIGAN Wallgate
WIGAN North Western
Bryn
Garswood
ST HELENS CENTRAL
Thatto Heath
Eccleston Park
Prescot
CITY LINE
Wavertree Technology Park
Edge Hill
Roby
Broad Green
HUYTON
Whiston
Rainhill
Lea Green
St Helens Junction
EARLESTOWN
Newton -le- Willows
Mossley Hill
West Allerton
Liverpool South Parkway
HUNTS CROSS
Hough Green
Sankey
Halewood
Widnes
WARRINGTON Central
WARRINGTON Bank Quay
RIVER MERSEY
RUNCORN
Runcorn East
Frodsham
Helsby
Acton Bridge
Hartford
Winsford
CREWE
Ince & Elton
Stanlow & Thornton
ELLESMERE PORT
Overpool
Little Sutton
Hooton
Capenhurst
Bache
CHESTER
Eastham Rake
Bromborough
Bromborough Rake
Spital
Port Sunlight
Bebington
Rock Ferry
Green Lane
Birkenhead Central
HAMILTON SQUARE
Conway Park
BIRKENHEAD
Birkenhead Park
Birkenhead North
Wallasey Village
Wallasey Grove Road
NEW BRIGHTON
BIDSTON
Leasowe
Moreton
Meols
Manor Road
Hoylake
WEST KIRBY
WIRRAL LINE
Upton
Heswall
Neston
Hawarden Bridge
Shotton
North Wales Coast
Wrexham
Wrexham Shrewsbury
Scotland The Lakes Morecambe Blackpool
East Lancashire
Bolton Manchester Manchester Airport
Manchester Airport Yorkshire
Manchester Yorkshire East Anglia
Shrewsbury Birmingham Cardiff London
Frequent bus links between CHESTER STATION and CHESTER CITY CENTRE free to rail passengers.
© Merseyside Passenger Transport Executive

EXPLORING the REGION

YOU are now 50 miles, as the Liver Bird flies, from the highest peak in Wales – Snowdon – and 65 miles from England's biggest mountain – Scafell Pike in the Lake District. Inbetween, there's a lot going on.

Clockwise: Caernarfon Castle, North Wales; Antony Gormley statues in a Crosby sunset; Chester – the Roman city; the famous Blackpool Tower; St Helens World of Glass

ANNUAL EVENTS

JANUARY

- RSPB BIG GARDEN BIRDWATCH

FEBRUARY

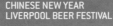

CHINESE NEW YEAR
LIVERPOOL BEER FESTIVAL

MARCH

- LIVERPOOL PERFORMING ARTS FESTIVAL
- LIVERPOOL HALF MARATHON
- ST DAVID'S DAY
- ST PATRICK'S DAY

JULY

- BROUHAHA INTERNATIONAL STREET FESTIVAL
- LIVERPOOL SUMMER POPS
- LIVERPOOL ARABIC ARTS FESTIVAL
- SOUTHPORT SUMMER CLASSICS
- BEATLES DAY

AUGUST

- CREAMFIELDS
- INTERNATIONAL BEATLES WEEK
- LIVERPOOL PRIDE
- MATHEW STREET FESTIVAL
- SLAVERY REMEMBRANCE DAY
- SOUTHPORT FLOWER SHOW

SEPTEMBER

- HERITAGE OPEN DAYS
- HOPE STREET FESTIVAL
- SOUTHPORT AIR SHOW
- LIVERPOOL FOOD & DRINK FESTIVAL

APRIL

- 3RD DEGREE MUSIC FESTIVAL, LIPA
- ST GEORGE'S DAY
- JOHN SMITH'S GRAND NATIONAL

MAY

- SOUTHPORT FOOD & DRINK FESTIVAL
- WRITING ON THE WALL FESTIVAL LIVERPOOL
- LIVERPOOL COMEDY FESTIVAL
- CROSBY MUSIC FESTIVAL
- HUB FESTIVAL
- SOUND CITY

JUNE

- LIVERPOOL TRIATHLON
- LIVERPOOL INTERNATIONAL TENNIS TOURNAMENT
- LORD MAYOR'S PARADE
- AFRICA OYÉ

OCTOBER

- FARMAGEDDON
- LIVERPOOL IRISH FESTIVAL
- SOUTHPORT COMEDY WEEK
- BRITISH MUSICAL FIREWORKS CHAMPIONSHIPS, SOUTHPORT

NOVEMBER

- INTERNATIONAL DADA FEST
- CITY OF LIVERPOOL FIREWORKS DISPLAY
- LIVERPOOL MUSIC WEEK
- HOMOTOPIA
- LIVERPOOL FOLK AND ROOTS FESTIVAL
- INTERNATIONAL GUITAR FESTIVAL, WIRRAL
- LIVERPOOL DESIGN FESTIVAL
- CHRISTMAS LIGHTS SWITCH-ON

DECEMBER

- LIVERPOOL CHRISTMAS MARKET
- NEW YEAR'S EVE FIREWORKS
- SANTA DASH 5K

FIRST CITY

THE word 'FIRST' is something we are proud of in the city. Here's a small selection of some of the groundbreaking achievements we are famous for . . .

If you are on holiday you are following in a fine tradition – Liverpool was the destination of the world's first package tour in 1845.

Need to take a photo? Liverpool provided the world's first photograph-developing and printing service in 1840.

Travel by train? This city showed off the world's first intercity passenger railway line built by Liverpool and Manchester Railway Company in 1830.

Ironically, on the same day the city saw the world's first railway fatality when the engine hit William Huskisson.

Nothing got in the way of progress however, when along came the first train shed, and first tunnel bored under a metropolis, and Edge Hill became the world's oldest-used train station.

Commerce was accelerating through the city and 1841 saw the first purpose-built office block. St George's Hall got the first air-conditioning system; Lime Street Station still has the world's largest single span roof.

Then there are the docks. The city's Old Dock was the world's first commercial enclosed wet dock when it was completed in 1715. Built on the mouth of the Pool, which gave Liverpool its name, the development of the dock saw a small village of 5,000 people transformed into a major port with 77,000 people 100 years later. It was buried in 1826 but has been preserved beneath the Liverpool One development and is now open as a public attraction.

The first tramway appeared at Liverpool Docks and the world's first steel ship, Ma Roberts, was built for Dr Livingstone's African exploration by the Laird Shipyard.

The Liverpool Overhead Railway opened in 1893 and was the world's first electrically-operated overhead railway.

A Liverpool-made gun fired the first shot of the American Civil War. The act of Surrender, by Captain James Waddell of the Shenandoah, was to the Mayor of Liverpool at the Town Hall, and the LAST official lowering of the Confederate flag was in the River Mersey in 1865.

The first disarmament campaign was by the Liverpool Peace Society in 1875.

At home, Liverpool pioneered in the world of social welfare, with the first public baths and wash house, the first nurse paid to look after the poor, the first Medical Officer – Doctor Duncan – and following the first slum clearance, the first provision of municipal housing.

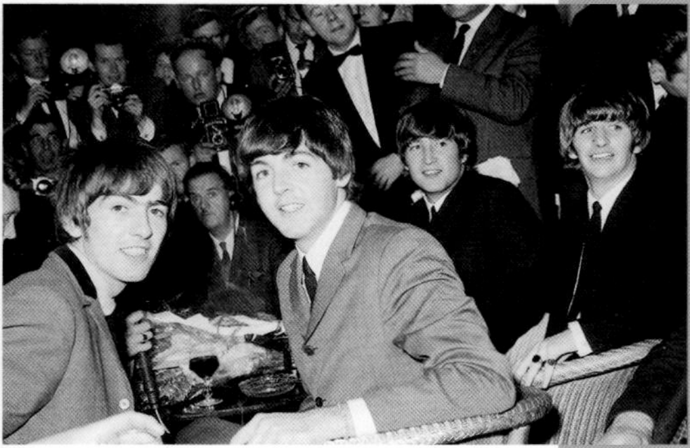

The Beatles were the first band to give fans printed lyrics on album sleeves, and the initial innovators of the now much imitated pop video.

First commercial public library, first Marine Biological station, purpose-built ambulance, first electric elevated urban railway, first radar lighthouse, first package holiday flight, the world's first oscillating sculpture, and the first and only group of musicians to achieve five diamond albums, signifying US sales of 10million or more.

SYMBOLS OF THE CITY

THE LIVER BIRD

The Liver Bird is the symbol of Liverpool. Two 18 ft tall birds stand on top of the Royal Liver Building – local legend has it that if the two birds were to fly away from each other the city would no longer exist! The bells of the Liver Building are part of the soundtrack to our city and mark each and every hour. It might come as a surprise to learn that there are no bells sounding when the clock strikes at all, just a series of piano strings played through an amplifier!

SUPERLAMBANANA

The iconic Superlambanana, designed by Japanese-based artist Taro Chiezo, has tended to roam the streets of Liverpool – its home for now is on the corner of Tithebarn Street and Vauxhall Road.

During 2008, 124 mini-replicas took to the streets for Go Superlambananas! It was such a success that eight 'Lambies' have now returned to Lime Street Station as a permanent legacy of Capital of Culture year.

DAY 1

IF money is no object, then stay over in style at the Hilton Liverpool. The Presidential Suite has a stunning view across the waterfront and is said to be the most expensive room in the city – a snip at around £790. Once you've got your bearings, start your sightseeing with the Albert Dock and Pier Head.

Unleash your digital camera on the Three Graces and board the Mersey Ferry for stunning views of the waterfront. Nip down to the Town Hall and Exchange Flags, then back down Castle Street and past the Brutalist-style Queen Elizabeth II Law Courts, for a teaser of Liverpool ONE and a drink looking over Chavasse Park. Then it's time to live the highlife with dinner at Panoramic, followed by people watching at trendy Newz Bar or partying in the outrageous and heaving Mathew Street.

A WEEKEND

DAY 2

Up Duke Street and past Jalon's Bridewell (with its famous Charles Dickens connection), to the Chinese Arch and the Anglican Cathedral, including Tracey Emin's Roman Standard at the Oratory. Pause for thought at The Hope Street suitcases by LIPA, or pop into The Phil for a pint, before visiting the Metropolitan Cathedral. Down the hill and past Lime Street Gateway, shoot the breeze in St John's Gardens, after you've had a peek inside St George's Hall, World Museum Liverpool and the Walker Art Gallery.

Recharge your batteries at The Bluecoat arts centre, the oldest Grade I listed building in central Liverpool, and take a wander up Stanley Street to meet Eleanor Rigby. Experience Liverpool's passion for football with a stadium tour at Anfield or Goodison Park, or get down to some serious shopping at Metquarter, Cavern Walks and Liverpool ONE. In the evening, you could catch a concert at The Phil, a gig at The Masque, a film at FACT or watch whatever's on at the Playhouse or Everyman. Then go for a cocktail at Alma De Cuba and a boogie at Heebiejeebies, Chibuku or Garlands.

in the CITY

DAY3

Grab some gifts at Stanley Dock's heritage market. Then head out of the city to Lark Lane, where you can buy a picnic hamper from The Moon and Pea deli and explore glorious Sefton Park and its palm house – the perfect way to end a weekend.

LIVERPOOL LOVES

- The old Liverpool accent – an Irish lilt, garnished with the singing voices of North Wales and the no-nonsense vowel sounds of Lancashire.
- Being able to dance your way through to the early hours in one of Liverpool's bars without having to pay over-inflated entry charges.
- Two Premiership football clubs only a short walk apart, plus Football League side Tranmere Rovers, just a quick train ride away.
- The largest collection of national museums and galleries outside London. On top of that, the Liverpool Biennial – held every two years – is the biggest art show in Britain.
- The world in one city – Liverpool's global heritage connects us with Africa, America, Israel, Haiti, China, Canada, France and Russia, to name but a few.
- Where else but Merseyside will strangers stop you while you are shopping to say how nice you look, or to tell you that you have left the price on your shoes?
- More Number One records than any other city. From the Beatles to Frankie Goes to Hollywood, Atomic Kitten to The Zutons, nobody knows how to write a great pop song like we do.
- Everyone knows your name in Liverpool – you're either La, Fella, Luv or Queen.

THE GUIDE

INSIDE the next 126 pages you'll find all you need to know about the latest tourist attractions, the bars and restaurants, the fashion and shopping and the best places to stay, as well as unbeatable coverage of Liverpool's arts and culture, entertainment, music and sport.

We'll show you where to go, what to see and what to do – walk this way . . .

ARCHITECTURE

EVERY guide taking tourists around Liverpool won't hesitate to mention that the city has two cathedrals – linked by a street called Hope.

Together they are part of our city, sung about in pubs to the chorus of Pete McGovern's anthem In My Liverpool Home – "We speak with an accent exceedingly rare, meet under a statue exceedingly bare, if you want a cathedral we've got one to spare".

The other fact that our guides proudly disseminate is that the gothic Anglican Liverpool Cathedral was designed by a Roman Catholic, Giles Gilbert Scott, while the unashamedly modern Roman Catholic Metropolitan Cathedral of Christ the King was designed by Frederick Gibberd, a Congregationalist.

The foundation stone of Liverpool Cathedral – the Anglican cathedral – was laid in 1904, but it was finally completed in 1978. In contrast, the building of its Roman Catholic counterpart was a much speedier affair, the bulk of the work, taking place between 1962 and 1967.

Hewn out of red Woolton sandstone, the Anglican Cathedral slowly emerged on the Liverpool skyline over three generations. Towering on its outcrop, the cathedral makes the observer gasp in wonderment.

It is very big, but never boring. With a footprint of 100,000sq ft, it occupies twice the space of St Paul's Cathedral in London. Other records the building holds include having the highest arches and vaults in the world. The organ, containing 10,000 pipes, is the largest of any church. The cathedral has the highest and heaviest ringing peal of bells in the world. It has drawn tourists from all over the world – and has been awarded a Marque of Excellence for making visitors feel welcome – with attractions including the launch of The Great Space, an interactive

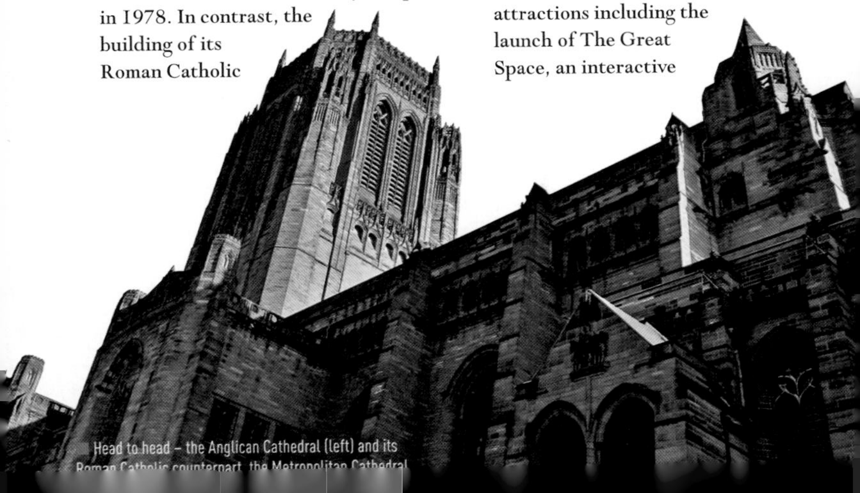

Head to head – the Anglican Cathedral (left) and its Roman Catholic counterpart, the Metropolitan Cathedral

HD experience allowing visitors to appreciate Giles Gilbert Scott's design.

While the huge funnel-like gothic tower of Liverpool Cathedral is easily picked out on the city's horizon, that of the smaller RC Metropolitan Cathedral is even more striking.

"Paddy's Wigwam," Arthur Dooley declared. Now nobody really knows if the redoubtable Dooley was the first in the city to so christen the Metropolitan Cathedral of Christ the King. But he certainly applied the description freely enough in conversation. Yet this building matured into the Liverpool scene, holding its own against the grander, neo-Gothic Anglican Cathedral at the other end of Hope Street.

Sitting on a podium covering Lutyens' crypt, the circular cathedral, built of concrete and Maltese limestone, reflected the 1960s liturgical trends and a fashion most often seen in the theatre in the round buildings. The theory is to bring the congregation of faithful as closely as possible to the mass.

In October 2003, the grand entrance and steps were opened together with a new Visitor Centre and the Piazza Restaurant.

This means the cathedral is now more in keeping with Sir Frederick Gibberd's original design, which envisaged a grand processional entrance looking on to Hope Street.

People are using the cathedrals more and feeling at home in them more. The annual Liverpool Beer Festival held in The Crypt of the Metropolitan Cathedral is the highest profile case of our cathedrals in commerce and showbiz, while the Anglican Cathedral has hosted slap-up dinners with comedians like John Bishop, as well as chat shows in The Nave with the likes of Janice Long and Mike McCartney.

Church art is not all stained glass windows and carved crucifixes these days. Liverpool's Anglican Cathedral is a case in point, having welcomed a number of high-profile artists and even commissioned some. Elizabeth Frink, Tracey Emin and Nicholas Charles Williams have all had their work exhibited there, while at the other end of Hope Street, an exhibition by Le Corbusier was one of the highlights of Capital of Culture year.

For those of you with an astrological or Pagan bent, it is said that a ley-line runs the length of Hope Street, and that this is the reason why the two cathedrals were built here.

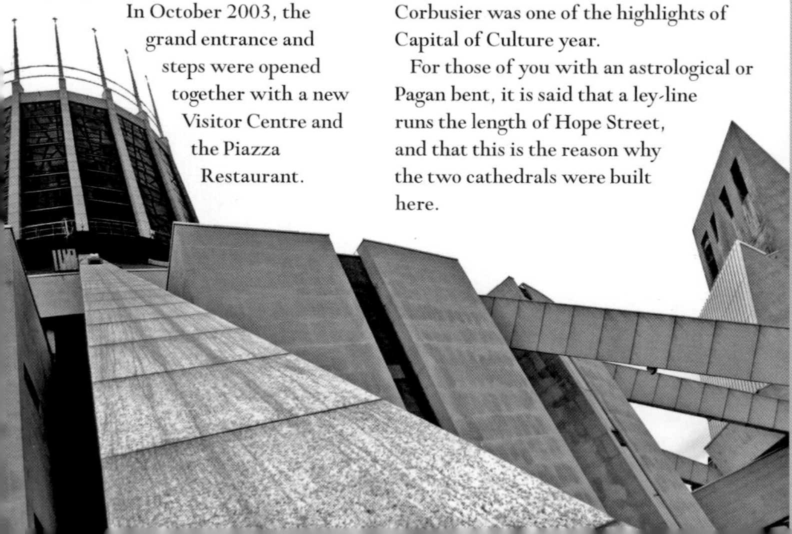

ALBERT DOCK
Edward Pavilion
Liverpool L3 4AG
www.albertdock.com

What remains of Liverpool's seafaring heritage is best seen at Albert Dock. This is one of the great monuments to Victorian engineering and now the largest English Heritage Grade I listed building complex. Ken Martin, a young lecturer at the then Liverpool Polytechnic, led the battle to save the Albert Dock from demolition in the 1970s when plans were drawn up to bulldoze the whole complex. He kicked up such a fuss the building, despite its dereliction, was spared. The £50m conversion work on Liverpool's Albert Dock turned it into the jewel in Liverpool's crown.

ALMA DE CUBA
St Peter's Church
Seel Street
Liverpool L1 4BH
0151 702 7394
www.alma-de-cuba.com

From the outside, it is a simple city church with no pretensions to grandeur. Step inside and the former St Peter's Church in one of Liverpool's Georgian quarters, is an architectural gem. After being unused for years, what was the oldest Roman Catholic church in Liverpool, dating from 1788, was not so much refurbished as reinvented as one of the city centre's hippest bars. Inside the church the altar remains, with its etched legend across the pediment with the words "Tu es Petrus", the famous quotation from Matthew 16:18 "Thou art Peter and upon this rock I will build my church".

THE BLUECOAT
School Lane
Liverpool L1 3BX
0151 702 5324
www.thebluecoat.org.uk

After a £12.5m refurbishment, the Bluecoat – the oldest arts centre in the country – reopened its doors in March 2008. At the heart of the project was the development of a wing, previously unused and once destroyed by fire in World War II. The join between the old school building – Grade I listed, dating back to 1717 – and the new, is one of the most special moments of contemporary architecture in Britain.

THE CHINESE ARCH
Nelson Street
Liverpool L1 5DN

The magnificent Chinese Arch at the top of Nelson Street, that constitutes the gateway to Chinatown, was designed by Mr Zhang and built in Shanghai by the South Linyi Garden Building Company. Standing at a height of 44 feet, it is the largest such arch outside China. Try and make it down for the Chinese New Year celebrations – and don't forget your wide-angle lens i[f] you want to take photos!

LIVERPOOL CATHEDRAL
St James Mount
Liverpool L1 7AZ
0151 798 6271
www.liverpoolcathedral.org.uk

A monument of superlatives, Liverpool's Anglican cathedral is the biggest in the UK and the fifth biggest on the planet. Visitors with a head for heights can enjoy the panoramic view of Liverpool from the cathedral's tower, also open for evening viewings until 8pm each Thursday from March to October.

LIVERPOOL METROPOLITAN CATHEDRAL
Mount Pleasant
Liverpool L3 5TZ
0151 709 9222
www.liverpoolmetrocathedral.org.uk

Even today 'Paddy's Wigwam' – the Roman Catholic Cathedral – has its critics, but it has rightly earned its place as an architectural gem. The immense, vertically-ribbed, cone-shaped lantern with its Crown of Thorns outline and stained glass (by John Piper) in a lace work-like lattice, is instantly recognisable. Lit from within, this 291ft high tower is every bit as exciting at night.

LIVERPOOL TOWN HALL
Dale Street
Liverpool L2 3SW
0151 236 5181
www.liverpool.gov.uk

Look out for the summer openings of Liverpool Town Hall. A Georgian jewel-box (1749-54) it was designed by the very fashionable John Wood the younger, of Bath, and James Wyatt. One favourite view is from the rear, when crossing the open space of Exchange Flags on a misty evening. From within, the chandeliers glint and the gilded plasterwork glows in the staterooms creating the most magical effect.

PRINCES ROAD SYNAGOGUE
Princes Road
Liverpool L8 1TG
0151 709 3431
www.princesroad.org

Designed and built – in a Moresque style – by architects W & G Audsley, and consecrated on September 3, 1874. It is a richly decorated and impressive building with a high, vaulted ceiling, beautifully carved and decorated. Certainly one of the most beautiful synagogues in Britain, and perhaps in Europe, and welcomes visitors from all over the world, whether of the Jewish Faith or not.

ST GEORGE'S HALL
St George's Place
Liverpool L1 1JJ
0151 225 6911
www.stgeorgesliverpool.co.uk

William Brown Street, home to the Walker Art Gallery, Liverpool Museum and Library, Wellington Column and Steble Fountain, is one world-class cityscape. Add to this the Neo-Classical splendour of St George's Hall and you have the most superb entrance to any city in the world.

The great hall, with its Minton floor and massive pipe organ, is St George's centrepiece, but the small concert room is the more enchanting. Inside the Heritage Centre you'll discover the original prison cells, newly-refurbished criminal court and judge's robing room as well as the stunning 169ft-long main Great Hall with the largest vaulted ceiling of its kind in Europe. The St George's Hall Balls, commissioned by Liverpool City Council, have become one of the most prestigious dance events in the country – a glamorous setting for a romantic Rumba.

THE THREE GRACES
Pier Head
Liverpool L3 1EG
One of the world's most famous skylines. Deservedly called the Three Graces, the name is only a recent appellation for a majestic trio of offices known for decades simply as the Pier Head buildings – The Royal Liver Building, The Cunard Building and the Port of Liverpool Building. With a rash of tall new buildings, it's probably best to take a trip on the ferry for the best view of these three iconic sisters.

WILLIAMSON TUNNELS
Heritage Centre
The Old Stable Yard
Smithdown Lane L7 3EE
0151 709 6868
A labyrinth of tunnels and underground caverns under the Edge Hill district of Liverpool. They were built in the first few decades of the 1800s under the control of a retired tobacco merchant called Joseph Williamson. The purpose of their construction is not known with any certainty. Theories range from philanthropy, offering work to the unemployed of the district, to religious extremism, the tunnels being an underground haven from a predicted Armageddon. Although some of the tunnels have been lost over the years, a lot of them still exist today, under what is now a residential area. Take a guided tour through a section of the network of tunnels and view exhibitions which depict the life and times of one of Liverpool's most eccentric characters.

OUT OF THE CITY

SPEKE HALL
GARDENS AND ESTATE
Liverpool L24 1XD
0844 800 4799
www.nationaltrust.org.uk
A rare Tudor manor house, in a most unusual setting. Half-timbered Tudor great hall featuring priest hole, Jacobean plasterwork and furniture, plus, below stairs, a Victorian kitchen and servants' hall. Don't miss the costumed guided tours, podcast tour and a walk in the woods and fragrant gardens.

BIRKENHEAD PRIORY
AND ST MARY'S TOWER
Priory Street
Birkenhead CH41 5JH
0151 666 4010
www.wirral.gov.uk
Merseyside's oldest building located by a former shipyard. Includes crenellations, pinnacles, a 12th-century vaulted chapter house, a museum in refectory and an undercroft. There are panoramic views from the restored Victorian church tower and a memorial to submariners lost when Thetis sank in 1939.

PORT SUNLIGHT
Wirral
www.portsunlight.org.uk
Across the water, the picturesque 19th century garden village of Port Sunlight, Wirral, is well worth a visit. Built by William Hesketh Lever for his soap factory workers – and named after his famous Sunlight soap – no fewer than 30 different architects were hired to create the unique style of the village. Although the majority of

houses are now privately owned, the historic village has changed little and still retains its original boundaries and mix of architectural styles, with no two pairs of houses alike. The Lady Lever Art Gallery, named in memory of Lever's beloved wife was a later addition, but now forms the centrepiece of the garden village. The fascinating story behind the creation of Port Sunlight itself can also be explored at the village's heritage centre.

CROWNE PLAZA HOTEL LIVERPOOL AIRPORT
Speke Aerodrome
Liverpool L24 8QD
With Grade II protected status, this hotel is a glamorous throwback to the days when Speke Airport opened in 1933. Many of the aerodrome's art deco features and fittings have been preserved in the hotel, just over a mile away from the new John Lennon Airport, including the Ambassador Suite, located in the terminal's control tower.

Secret underground city

"HEY, man, dig those crazy vibes," whispered the cool cat in shades way back in the 1950s, as his slip-on shoes shuffled down the steps into a jive cellar throbbing with young life – where the musicians with unsunned faces were plucking strings and blowing horns.

And "dig" is the important word here. For, although Liverpudlians these days look with kindly eyes on the new buildings piercing the clouds over the waterfront, their instincts have always taken them underground. But understanding the subterranean city of years gone-by is essential to the regeneration of today.

Liverpool lies on durable sandstone, which provides a strong base and can also be dug comparatively easily. Our subterranean city is proportionately the biggest in Britain. The jazz and skiffle crazes of the 1950s gave the cellars a new vibrancy. Of course, on a larger scale, cellars were opened to the public as clubs and music venues, most famously The Cavern, on Mathew Street.

Underground Liverpool was honeycombed with tunnels, culverts, basements and passages. Most prominent of these were the railway tunnels joining Edge Hill with the docks at Wapping (1827) and Waterloo (1849). These were followed in 1880 by the railway tunnel under the Mersey linking Liverpool's James Street station with Birkenhead Hamilton Square. Then came the road tunnels from Liverpool to Birkenhead (1934) and Wallasey (1971).

And we haven't yet mentioned Liverpool's most celebrated king of the underworld. The Mole of Edge Hill was a character that would be hard to invent, yet is so peculiarly appropriate to Merseyside's folklore.

In the early 19th century, Joseph Williamson (1769-1840), a tobacco merchant and philanthropist, ordered a labyrinth of tunnels to be dug in an area to the east of the Metropolitan Cathedral – quite why remains unknown. Was it simply to provide work and wages for local men? Could they have been designed as shelters for people escaping some future Armageddon? Today, his inexplicable creation is the subject of one of our most unusual future tourist attractions. In fact, it could be one of Britain's strangest visitor sights.

David Charters

CHINATOWN

LIVERPOOL once had the largest and oldest Chinese community outside mainland China and was officially twinned with Shanghai in 2000, cementing our cultural and business links.

The magnificent Chinese Arch was built in Shanghai, then dismantled and shipped to Liverpool. It was then reconstructed by eight craftsmen who worked every day for three months.

Feng Shui Masters carefully selected the site of the arch, to ensure good fortune to the local community, and it was unveiled in September 2000.

There are 200 dragons carved into the arch, 12 of which are pregnant as this is considered a sign of very good fortune indeed. The five colours relate to the five Chinese elements of earth (yellow), wood (green), metal (white), water (black) and fire (red).

The Chinese characters that appear in the panel in the centre of the main span of the arch translate as – reading from right to left naturally – 'Middle Kingdom', which was the ancient name for China.

In the heart of Chinatown is the Pagoda – which it is not! However, this otherwise fairly ordinary building is the local Community Centre, where Chinese culture is celebrated, preserved and warmly shared.

Chinese New Year is celebrated with tremendous enthusiasm every year throughout Chinatown, centred on Nelson Street.

The Dancing Dragons, the Lion Dance, the fire-crackers, fairground rides, food-stalls and Bazaar-like atmosphere always attract hundreds of people to join in the fun.

In 2010, Liverpool's Chinese New Year spectacular celebrated the Year of the Tiger and the tenth anniversary of the twinning with Shanghai, before heading to the World Expo 2010 in China's largest city.

There are many delicious restaurants in Chinatown, offering a wide range of gastronomic experiences, some of which require a very adventurous spirit!

Ken Pye

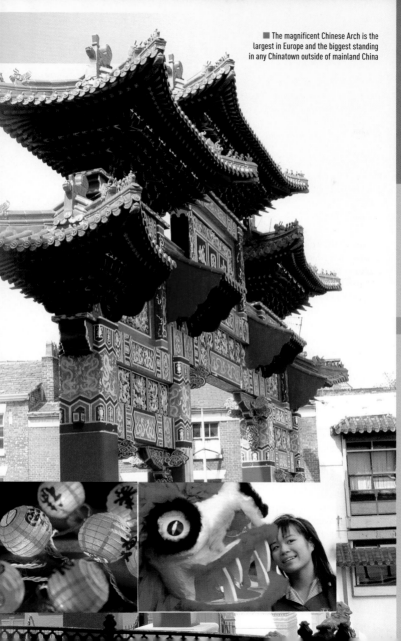

The magnificent Chinese Arch is the largest in Europe and the biggest standing in any Chinatown outside of mainland China

If walls could talk

LIVERPOOL retains a remarkable heritage of not only landmark buildings, but lesser-known, equally priceless structures.

One of the most dignified hidden gems of Liverpool's heritage is the Cenotaph (1926) on St George's Plateau. Unusually long and low for a war memorial, its shape is designed to reflect St George's Hall behind. After extensive restoration by National Museums' Liverpool Conservation Centre, the superb bronze panels by Herbert Tyson Smith can be seen in their full glory.

Down on The Strand, near the Pier Head, is the George's Dock Vent, a fine art deco building designed by Herbert Rowse, to ventilate the Mersey Tunnel.

The sculptures by Capstick and Thompson include the black basalt Night and Day (ie the tunnel never closes) and Speed, said to be a stylised representation of record-breaking aviatrix Amy Johnson.

This the public can view during events such as Civic Trust open days. The White Star Building on James Street is not as grandiose as its Cunard near neighbour, but is a highly distinctive building, with its "streaky bacon" exterior of red brick and Portland stone. From its balconies was shouted the news of the company's ill-fated Titanic to local families of crew members involved in the tragedy.

Large numbers of Scandinavian sailors passed through Liverpool, with 200 ships from there docking in the port during 1875. Sweden decided a Lutheran church was necessary,

building the Gustaf Adolfs Kyrka, in 1884.

This Grade II listed church incorporates Nordic timber church details and was copied for the Swedish Church in Hamburg.

Our Lady and St Nicholas is Liverpool's parish church and also the sailors' church. Once the Mersey lapped at its churchyard, until pushed back by the road and docks.

Overlooked by many, Oriel Chambers, Water Street, built in 1864, is one of the most important buildings in the world. It is the grand-daddy of architecture's Modern Movement with large glass oriel windows hung on the building's frame.

Nearby, also on Water Street, the former Bank of Liverpool HQ has two large bronze tiger heads on its doors, once rubbed for good luck by Lascar Indian seamen, who came from an area of man-eating tigers.

To experience a flavour of old Liverpool you should ascend to Rodney Street, Hope Street and Abercromby Square. This is where the great and good of the town lived, up above the roar and stench of the working port that provided their fortunes. Rodney Street in particular is exquisite, and was once known as "The Harley Street of the North" because so many medical consultants had rooms there. Soon its style attracted the mercantile wealthy, perhaps the most impressive being the Gladstone family – William Gladstone, four times Prime Minister was born at No 62.

Peter Elson

Your pass to Access All historic Areas

FEW of us can resist getting a glimpse of life behind closed doors.

We've all passed houses or other buildings which reek of character and wondered what it was like inside. Those so afflicted will relish the invite to legitimately poke around such properties during Heritage Open Days, held over four days in September.

The annual event celebrates England's fantastic architecture and culture by offering free access to properties that are usually closed to the public or normally charge for admission. Buildings of every age, style and function throw open their doors, ranging from castles to factories, town halls to tithe barns, parish churches to Buddhist temples.

Liverpool always has a marvellous array of open venues to visit. The likes of the Ancient Chapel of Toxteth, George's Dock ventilation station, Daniel Adamson steam tug tender, Liverpool Medical Institution, Edward Chambré Hardman's House, the Athenaeum and the Cunard Building have all taken part in the national Heritage Open Days event, joined by popular venues like the Adelphi Hotel, Williamson Tunnels, Liverpool Town Hall, St George's Hall, the World Museum and the ruined Rodney Street church of St Andrew's.

Patrick Burke, of English Heritage North West, says: "This is the free event with something for everyone. It involves 40,000 people across Britain, and it's a bit different from the normal experience of visiting places. These volunteers often speak with unbridled enthusiasm from the heart, which brings places alive."

Visit: www.heritageopendays.org.uk

STATELY HOMES

Knowsley Hall, one of the largest Georgian mansions in the country

MERSEYSIDE isn't famed for its great stately homes and halls, but in truth there is as rich an architectural variety as anywhere, with plenty to delight the eye.

Not all are open to the public and their opening times may be seasonal, so please check before venturing off on your travels. The three biggest are the half-timbered Speke Hall, and the great piles of Knowsley and Croxteth. Between and around these are gems like Stanlawe Grange, in Grassendale, dating from 1291 and the oldest building in Liverpool. Or there's the jewel of Sudley House, the only complete furnished example of a Liverpool shipping magnate's home.

Speke Hall is everyone's idea of the

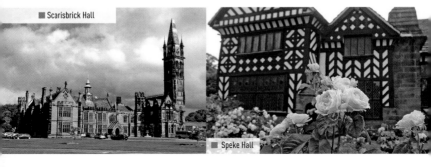

Scarisbrick Hall
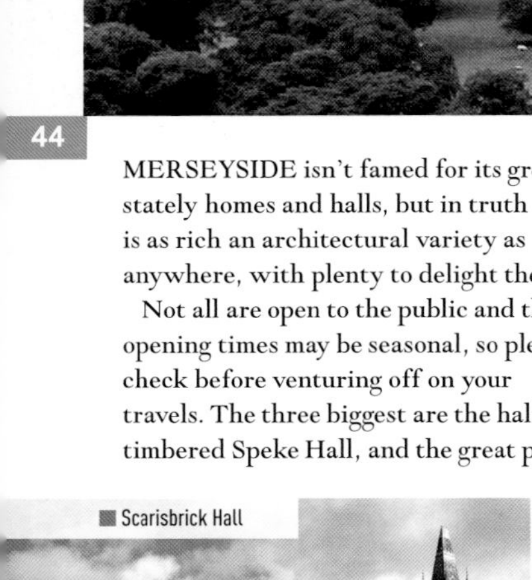

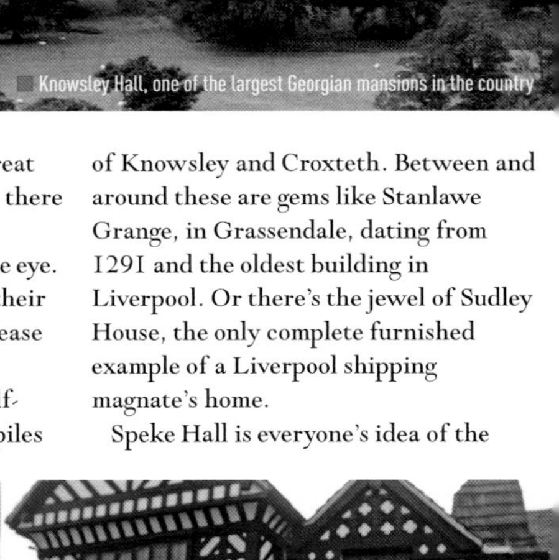
Speke Hall

dream Tudor house, a great undulating range of black and white magpie half-timbering and plaster in-fill, punctuated by gables and brick chimney stacks. Croxteth Hall, in West Derby, only dates from 40 years after Speke, and was built by Richard Molyneux, whose family went on to greater things as the Earls of Sefton.

The Molyneux/Sefton's great rivals were the Stanleys, or Earls of Derby, who are still very much alive and kicking. Their home, Knowsley Hall, exists in an estate that is more akin to the Cotswolds than the adjacent Liverpool urban conurbation.

Home of the Derbys since the 14th century, the Hall itself is one of the largest Georgian mansions in the country. No longer the home of the Stanley family, it has been restored and converted for functions, private events and luxury breaks.

One of Liverpool's foremost merchant princes was William Roscoe (1753-1831), who at his peak inhabited Allerton Hall, at Calderstones. Originally an Elizabethan house, it was remodelled to reflect changing tastes in the 18th and 19th century. Roscoe fell in love with the Italian Renaissance, although he never visited Italy, and sent his agents there to buy illuminated manuscripts and paintings. He particularly liked the Primitive painting styles and these now form an important part of the Walker Art Gallery collection.

Almost unknown is Greenbank House, of 1815, in Liverpool's Green Bank Park, home of the Rathbone banking family from 1787. The main block is a graceful marriage of Georgian and Gothic styles, but its most important historic feature is the delightful lace-like cast-iron screen on the garden facade. The building was

The splendour of Knowsley

converted in 1964 into a university club for staff and students.

For the really flamboyant counterpoint, we need to look towards Scarisbrick (pronounced Scazebrick) Hall. On land occupied by the Scarisbrick family since the time of Richard the Lionheart, arose an edifice that is one of England's finest Gothic Revival buildings. Completed in 1867, Scarisbrick Hall with its 100ft-high tower is a West Lancashire landmark. Created by Charles Scarisbrick, one of Lancashire's wealthiest men, it resembles the Houses of Parliament, unsurprising as the architect Augustus Welby Pugin helped design the Palace of Westminster.

Today, Scarisbrick Hall is occupied by an independent school and there is no public access apart from infrequent guided tours, but the building is spectacular.

ARTS & CULTURE

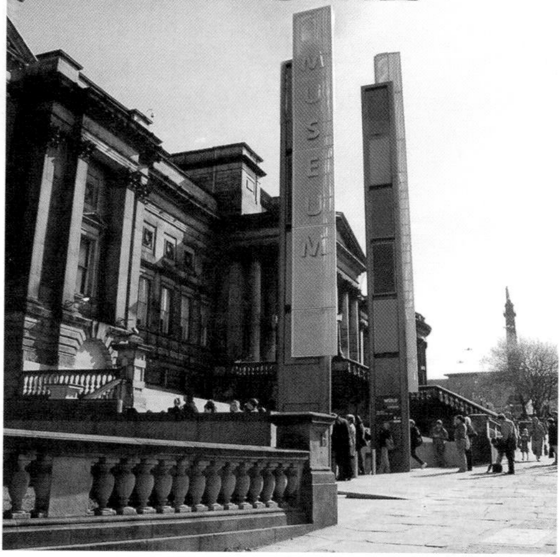

MUSEUMS

INTERNATIONAL SLAVERY MUSEUM
Albert Dock
Liverpool L3 4AX
0151 478 4499
www.liverpoolmuseums.org.uk
The International Slavery Museum explores both the historical and contemporary aspects of slavery, addressing the many legacies of the slave trade and telling stories of bravery and rebellion amongst the enslaved people. These are stories which have been largely untold.

LIVERPOOL WAR MUSEUM
1-3 Rumford Street
Liverpool L2 3SZ
0151 227 2008
www.liverpoolwarmuseum.co.uk
Western Approaches offers one of the most unique and realistic glimpses at what life was like for the people in the thick of it, behind the scenes of the Battle of the Atlantic – this cavernous, underground control room (with its 7-foot thick roof and 3-foot thick walls) was bomb proof, gas proof and proved to be the most successful tool in the British emerging victorious in World War II, before its closure in August 1945. Today, the wartime bunker is open to the general public and its cold, hard atmosphere serve as a chilling reminder of the price you pay in a war.

MERSEYSIDE MARITIME MUSEUM
Albert Dock
Liverpool L3 4AQ
0151 478 4499
www.liverpoolmuseums.org.uk
Discover Liverpool's central role in centuries at sea as the gateway to the new world. Highlights include a gallery about the Titanic, ship models and the Life at Sea display, telling the story of The Merchant Navy. New for 2010, tours of Liverpool's revolutionary Old Dock, the world's first commercial enclosed wet dock, preserved in Liverpool ONE.

MR HARDMAN'S PHOTOGRAPHIC STUDIOS
59 Rodney Street
Liverpool L1 9EX
0151 709 6261
www.nationaltrust.org.uk
Former home and studio of the renowned Liverpool photographer Edward Chambré Hardman, who lived in the Georgian terraced house from 1947-1988. Darkroom, studio, living quarters, photographic display focusing on Liverpool area and costume tours. Admission by timed ticket only – advance booking recommended.

MUSEUM OF LIVERPOOL
Pier Head Liverpool
www.liverpoolmuseums.org.uk
At the core of the new £72m Museum of Liverpool are the people of Liverpool, their triumphs and tribulations. The new building on the Pier Head will include the atrium, Little Liverpool children's gallery on the ground floor and the huge second floor themed galleries – Creative City and People's City – with their stunning views over the Three Graces and the Albert Dock.

NATIONAL CONSERVATION CENTRE
Whitechapel
Liverpool L1 6HZ
0151 478 4999
www.liverpoolmuseums.org.uk
Most conservation work goes on behind the scenes, but here you can get expert advice on caring for your own treasures. Find out how everything from Egyptian mummies to motorbikes are preserved and restored in the interactive Reveal gallery and laboratory.

VICTORIA GALLERY AND MUSEUM
Victoria Building
Brownlow Hill
Liverpool L69 3DR
0151 794 2348
www.liv.ac.uk/vgm/
The VGM collection includes early English watercolours, ceramics, fine art and works by 20th century artists, including Jacob Epstein, Lucien Freud and Elizabeth Frink. The museum exhibits include sea creatures and animal skeletons from an early 20th century zoology museum, fossils of footprints from extinct dinosaur ancestors, a display of calculators from the 19th century to the present day and X-rays from the beginning of X-ray technology.

WORLD MUSEUM
William Brown Street
Liverpool L3 8EN
0151 478 4393
www.liverpoolmuseums.org.uk
This museum's magnificent collections are brought to life through live performances and talks. Highlights include the aquarium, Treasure House Theatre, Clore Natural History Centre, Bug House, World Cultures gallery, as well as exhibits on ancient Egypt, Greece and Rome, dinosaurs, fossils, space and time, and a planetarium.

OUT OF TOWN

BIRKENHEAD TRAMWAY & WIRRAL TRANSPORT MUSEUM
1 Taylor Street
Birkenhead CH41 1BG
0151 647 2128
www.wirral.gov.uk
Historic home of Europe's first tramway. Take the tramway from Woodside Visitor Centre to The Old Colonial pub at the Taylor Street terminus. Take a guided tour of the Heritage Centre housing a collection of restored and part-restored buses and trams.

NATIONAL WATERWAYS MUSEUM ELLESMERE PORT
South Pier Road
Ellesmere Port CH65 4FW
0151 355 5017
www.nwm.org.uk/ellesmere
Unlock the wonders of our waterways – with its delightful waterside setting, flotillas of historic boats and fascinating displays housed in fine Victorian buildings.

PORT SUNLIGHT MUSEUM AND GARDEN VILLAGE
3 King George's Drive
Port Sunlight CH62 5DX 0151 644 4800
www.portsunlightvillage.com
Meet the village's creator 'Soap King' William Hesketh Lever, find out about the architects who designed the houses, and experience what it was like to work here during the Edwardian and Victorian periods.

SUDLEY HOUSE
Mossley Hill Road
Liverpool L18 8BX
0151 724 3245
www.liverpoolmuseums.org.uk
Built in the 1830s, Sudley House is now a beguiling gallery of paintings and furniture which give an excellent idea of the quality of life enjoyed by the rich in the 19th century.

GALLERIES

OPEN EYE GALLERY
28-32 Wood Street
Liverpool L1 4AQ
0151 709 9460
Long-established, much-loved and showcasing innovative and challenging photography and media art with an international pedigree. Open Eye Gallery is moving to larger premises on the Liverpool waterfront – the new space will be launched in autumn 2010. In the meantime you can still catch occasional exhibitions and events at the original Wood Street base.

RIBA MILK AND SUGAR
The Tea Factory
82 Wood Street
Liverpool L1 4DQ
0151 707 4380
www.milk-and-sugar.co.uk
A unique events venue and gallery space in Liverpool's lively and cosmopolitan Ropewalks district.

STATIC GALLERY
23 Roscoe Lane
Liverpool L1 9JD
An industrial yet cosy vibe, this venue hosts art exhibitions and live bands, as well as a wonderful café.

TATE LIVERPOOL
Albert Dock
Liverpool L3 4BB
0151 702 7400
www.tate.org.uk/liverpool
Otherwise known as the National Collection of Modern Art in the North of England . . .

Major exhibitions have included the Turner Prize 2007; Gustav Klimt: Painting, Design and Modern Life in Vienna 1900; and Summer of Love: Art of the Psychedelic Era. In the summer of 2010 a major exhibition called Picasso: Peace and Freedom will reveal a fascinating new insight into the artist's life. Tate Liverpool continues to play an active role in the Liverpool Biennial. Entry is free except for major exhibitions.

THE GALLERY
First floor, The Courtyard
41 Stanhope Street
Liverpool L8 5RE
0151 709 2442
www.thegalleryliverpool.co.uk
The Gallery occupies the entire upper floor of the industrial premises of John O'Keeffe & Son Ltd, well known local signmakers and engravers, which is just off Parliament Street. This venue promotes a range of artistic approaches and showcases home-grown local talent.

UNIVERSITY OF LIVERPOOL ART GALLERY
3 Abercromby Square
Liverpool L69 7WY
0151 794 2348
www.liv.ac.uk
The Art Gallery houses permanent displays of fine and decorative art from the University's collections. Visitors can see selections from the Sydney Jones collection of early English watercolours, paintings by Joseph Wright of Derby and JMW Turner, and a rare group of oil paintings by the seminal American wildlife artist John James Audubon.

VIEW TWO GALLERY
23 Mathew Street
Liverpool L2 6RE
0151 236 9444
www.viewtwogallery.co.uk
Three floors of wonderfully eclectic work by local and global artists in an informal venue. There is a licensed bar too – call in on a Saturday afternoon and enjoy a complimentary drink while viewing the artworks.

WALKER ART GALLERY
William Brown Street
Liverpool L3 8EL
0151 478 4199
www.liverpoolmuseums.org.uk
The first British public art gallery and one of the finest in Europe. The full-length Henry VIII portrait (attributed to a follower of Hans Holbein) is thought to have belonged to his favourite wife Jane Seymour, while William Hogarth's 1745 painting of David Garrick as Richard III captures the Marlon Brando of his day in full method-acting mode. The Tinted Venus, whose flesh-coloured body, blue eyes and golden hair caused a scandal when shown in London in 1862, is the beloved creation of local Neo-Classical sculptor John Gibson. Other must-see works include Monet's Break-up of the Ice on the Seine, David Hockney's cheeky 1967 Moores winner Peter Getting out of Nick's Pool and Dante's Dream from 1897 by Gabriel Rossetti.

OUT OF TOWN

ATKINSON ART GALLERY
Lord Street
Southport PR8 1DH
0151 934 2110
www.atkinsonfriends.org.uk
Nineteenth and 20th century watercolours and oil paintings, sculptures and contemporary art by such luminaries as Henry Moore, LS Lowry and AJ Munnings.

CORNERSTONE GALLERY
Hope University
17 Shaw Street
Liverpool L6 1HP
0151 291 3997
www.hope.ac.uk
Set at the grand entrance of Liverpool Hope's Cornerstone Campus, the gallery exists as an autonomous space with a prime aim of assisting and promoting new and emerging artists within the North West.

LADY LEVER ART GALLERY
Port Sunlight Village
Wirral CH62 5EQ
0151 478 4136
The Lady Lever Art Gallery, named in memory of Lever's beloved wife, was a later addition to Port Sunlight, but now forms the centrepiece of the garden village. The gallery houses a superb collection of pre-Raphaelite masterpieces including works by Millais, Ford Madox Brown and Rossetti, dramatic landscapes by Constable and Turner, as well as Wedgwood china, tapestries, Greek vases and Roman sculpture, with plenty of sensuous nudes on display. There is also a room dedicated to works connected with Napoleon, reflecting one of Leverhulme's great interests, and a display of the familiar paintings first used to advertise Sunlight soap. The fascinating story behind the creation of Port Sunlight itself can also be explored in more depth at the village's heritage centre.

METAL
Edge Hill Station
Tunnel Road
Liverpool L7 6ND
0151 707 2277
www.metalculture.com
A cluster of Grade II-listed buildings at the world's oldest working mainline station, transformed into artists' studios and exhibition space. The five-year renovation project was led by Liverpool-born Jude Kelly, director of London's Southbank Centre.

WILLIAMSON ART GALLERY AND MUSEUM
Slatey Road
Birkenhead L43 4UE
0151 652 4177
www.wirral.gov.uk
Houses the vast majority of Birkenhead's collection of artistic masterpieces. On display are Victorian oil paintings, English watercolours, Liverpool Porcelain and DellaBir Robbia Pottery. Local history exhibits and ship models also feature in this art gallery dating from the 1920s.

THE BLACK-E
Great George Street
Liverpool L1 5EW
0151 709 5109
www.theblack-e.co.uk

After a £6m restoration project was completed in 2009, the North West's only in-the-round auditorium reopened its doors for public performances of dance, drama and music. The arts organisation, formerly known as the Blackie, describes the Great George Street centre as a "new building within old walls". It was first christened the Blackie because in the 1960s the church was covered in a century's worth of smoke and grime. In 1987, the filthy, black-stained exterior of the building was thoroughly cleaned, but it retained its nickname.
Now known as the Black-E, the Grade II former congregational chapel at the gateway to Chinatown boasts five floors of arts spaces, gallery, offices, cafeteria, crèche and changing rooms. It includes the lower ground floor Chamber Theatre, a first-floor main space with a 27ft high ceiling and two levels of balconies and roof level offices, plus meeting rooms. The showcase, three storey high main space, which has balcony railings designed by artist Giuseppe Lund together with Liverpool people, can seat some 550 people.

THE BLUECOAT
School Lane
Liverpool L1 3BX
0151 702 5324
www.thebluecoat.org.uk

Lauded by the critics, visited by Yoko and welcomed back into the hearts of the city's creative types like a long lost family member, the new Bluecoat has found the winning formula: how to create an arts venue that's as much a social meeting place as a cultural melting pot.
The five-year £12.5m refurbishment of the Bluecoat resulted in the replacement of an entire wing of the building flattened during the Blitz, providing within three extra art galleries, a 200-seat theatre space and a splendid new restaurant. The 'secret' inner garden – a traditional haven for office workers at lunchtime – has been fully restored, as have the artists' studios of old, including the foundry and workshop, once occupied by the legendary sculptor George Herbert Tyson Smith. Dancers, artists, musicians and writers are all thrown together in this new hothouse.

THE CAPSTONE
Liverpool Hope University
Shaw Street
Liverpool L3 8QB
0151 709 3789
www.hope.ac.uk

The Capstone is Liverpool Hope's new Centre for Music, Performance and Innovation. Opened in March 2010, it boasts 10 music practice rooms, three music studios, three music technology laboratories, teaching rooms, music therapy rooms and an exhibition gallery. After hours it is open with public shows in the Hope Theatre. The Capstone, funded with assistance from the North West Development Agency and the Higher Education Funding Council for England (HEFCE), it is one of only three Steinway Schools in the UK. The European Opera Centre, another partner of the University, will be based at the Capstone while the RLPO's contemporary Ensemble 10/10 will also perform there.

CONTEMPORARY URBAN CENTRE
41–51 Greenland Street
Liverpool L1 0BS
0151 708 3510
www.contemporaryurbancentre.org
Set in the heart of the emerging 'Independent Arts Quarter' of Liverpool, the Contemporary Urban Centre has much to offer city centre culture vultures. It boasts a 750-capacity auditorium, galleries, dance studio, a cinema, restaurants, café and a beer hall – surely making it a contender for the title of the Southbank Centre of Liverpool. Yet the Contemporary Urban Centre is probably something of a mystery to many in the city, despite a staggering 170,000sq ft of space behind its seven-storey red brick walls with its name emblazoned in giant letters along the top. The Contemporary Urban Centre is a big lady. The venue has hosted a number of events including the Liverpool Art Prize, Biennial, Nordic Arts Festival NICE and the launch of Brouhaha (the arts organisation has offices in the building).

FACT
88 Wood Street
Liverpool L1 4DQ
0151 707 4464
www.fact.co.uk
Part cinema, part art gallery and part performance space, FACT is something of a Liverpool institution. The FACT bar is a great place to hang out too. Along with fortnightly film quizzes, it hosts monthly poetry evenings and, because it is fully licensed throughout the building, you can enjoy your drinks in the cinemas. Bliss.

ST LUKE'S CHURCH
Leece Street
Liverpool L1 2TR
www.myspace.com/lunchatstlukes
Liverpool's pioneering Urban Strawberry Lunch combo are behind the regeneration of this much-loved, but often ignored building, referred to by Scousers as 'the bombed-out church'. This noble pile, blitzed in 1941, has been given a new lease of life with exhibitions, unplugged gigs, poetry, theatre and film screenings. Visit a neglected Liverpool treasure.

THEATRE

A rapturous applause at The Playhouse

IT is rumoured that Shakespeare once came to Liverpool.

He said that 'all the world's a stage' and he travelled the country to see it and perform. According to folklore, he enjoyed a visit to Prescot and met its creative peoples. We no doubt made him welcome.

But Shakespeare's words have a particular resonance for Liverpool, a city where every other taxi driver is a closet playwright, where every schoolchild a budding performer and where every available space – from waterfronts to disused warehouses to cathedrals – is a possible stage.

Actors, writers, comedians, directors, musicians – Liverpool produces them all in abundance, and over more than two centuries a huge number of venues have sprung up to sate the population's appetite for live theatre.

Many of those venues no longer exist, but Liverpool can still boast one of the largest concentrations of theatres for a city its size in the UK. From the 2,400-seat Empire to the 80-seat Actors' Studio, from the Playhouse to the Paul McCartney Auditorium, they offer something for everyman. And every woman, of course.

Added to that, the wider Merseyside region as a whole boasts a wide collection of theatres from the Theatre Royal in St Helens to the newly-renovated Floral Pavilion at New Brighton. It's that rich mix that makes Liverpool and Merseyside a vibrant theatrical hub.

Catherine Jones

Pauline Daniels, The Actors' Studio

THE ACTORS' STUDIO
36 Seel Street
Liverpool L1 4BE
0151 709 9034
www.theliverpoolactorsstudio.com

Tucked away at the bottom of Seel Street is what many are hailing as the saviour of fringe theatre. Set in a building steeped in artistic history that was once home to the renowned sculptor Arthur Dooley, week after week this secret well of talent stages cutting edge theatre from straight plays to musicals, comedy to variety.

THE EVERYMAN
13 Hope Street
Liverpool L1 9BH
0151 709 4776
www.everymanplayhouse.com

The old Hope Hall, as it was called, prides itself on giving new writers a voice – Willy Russell and Alan Bleasdale matured there and actors such as Julie Walters, Bill Nighy and Pete Postlethwaite honed their craft in this much respected iconic theatre. The next chapter in the story will be a major capital £28m redevelopment which will equip the Everyman and the Playhouse fully for the 21st century.

THE LIVERPOOL EMPIRE
Lime Street
Liverpool L1 1JE
0151 708 3200
www.liverpoolempire.org.uk

The grade II listed Empire Theatre we know today was opened in March 1925, rebuilt and enlarged to an American design to become the most up-to-date theatre in the provinces. It had the widest auditorium in Europe, and a capacity of 2,381. In the 60s and 70s the theatre played host to big names in the music industry, not least the Beatles, while it has also hosted a number of Royal Command and Royal Variety performances. In 1998 the theatre underwent the start of an £11m refurbishment, and the atrium annex was completed in 2002. It is one of the largest two-tier theatres in the country and the home for touring and home-grown musicals, comedy shows and similar entertainment.

NEPTUNE THEATRE
Hanover Street
Liverpool L1

The Neptune closed in 2005 for refurbishment with an estimated reopening date of 2007, but complications and disagreements over rent delayed work. It is hoped the building will be restored and working again at some point in 2010.

THE PLAYHOUSE
Williamson Square
Liverpool L1 1EL
0151 709 4776
www.everymanplayhouse.com

Built in 1986 as the Star Music Hall, the Playhouse became a full-time repertory theatre in 1911 and was the oldest rep in the country until 1999, when the Playhouse and Everyman joined together under a single management, taking the city's theatre forward. Now it welcomes the best of big and small touring companies, specialising in bold and creative interpretations of the very best drama.

The Redgrave Room at The Playhouse

THE ROYAL COURT
1 Roe Street
Liverpool L1 1HL
0870 787 1866
www.royalcourtliverpool.co.uk

The Royal Court has once again become a home for theatrical productions, often home-grown comedy plays performed by an informal "repertory" company of actors. The red-bricked venue has a capacity of 1,186 seats and plays by Willy Russell (pictured) still win sell-out audiences.

There are currently plans to regenerate the Royal Court for the 21st century, updating facilities for audiences and performers and creating a new entrance and rooftop extension.

UNITY THEATRE
1 Hope Place
Liverpool L1 9BG
0151 709 6502
www.unitytheatreliverpool.co.uk

The Unity Theatre celebrates its 30th anniversary at its Hope Street base in 2010. It was originally founded in Mount Pleasant in 1937 as the Merseyside Left Theatre, part of a national theatre movement which aimed to

make theatre accessible to "the great mass of the people". One of the best-loved theatres in Liverpool, The Unity has maintained its reputation for staging innovative, high-quality work, encouraging new writing and supporting new companies. Patrons include actors Ian Hart, David Morrissey and Andrew Lancel.

OUT OF TOWN

THE BRINDLEY
High Street
Runcorn WA7 1BG
0151 907 8360
www.thebrindley.org.uk

CITADEL ARTS CENTRE
Waterloo Street
St Helens WA10 1PX
01744 735 436
www.citadel.org.uk

GLADSTONE THEATRE
Gladstone Hall
Wirral CH62 4XB
0151 643 8757
www.gladstonetheatre.org.uk

FLORAL PAVILION
Marine Promenade
New Brighton CH45 2JS
0151 666 0000
www.floralpavilion.com

ROSE THEATRE
Edge Hill University
Ormskirk L39 4QP
01695 584480
www.edgehill.ac.uk/rosetheatre

SOUTHPORT THEATRE
The Promenade
Southport PR9 0DZ
01704 500036
www.visitsouthport.com

That's entertainment!

LIVERPOOL loves to be entertained . . . and to entertain. So, ladies and gentleman, please give a big round of applause to the following key venues that cater for all tastes, genres and ages.

The Empire on Lime Street is one of the biggest provincial theatres outside London. From Blood Brothers to Oklahoma, Welsh National Opera to Ballet, it is also a popular venue for rock and pop concerts and stand-up comedians. Even Happy Days star Henry Winkler (pictured with Natasha Hamilton) relished his time as Captain Hook in the pantomime Peter Pan.

Over in Roe Street, another venue has enjoyed consistently loyal audiences. Ken Dodd, the King of Comedy, says The Royal Court is one of his favourite theatres and that's quite a compliment from a man who has played more UK venues than any other performer. Built in 1938 'the Court' as it's known has a unique Art Deco style. It has gone through more changes of direction and scenery than many of the productions it stages.

In 1980 the ailing theatre was taken over by two former Liverpool taxi drivers and it became a venue for rock and pop performances from the likes of REM, David Bowie, Wings and Oasis.

Five years ago the Rawhide Comedy Club took over the venue – the forward-looking managers made a move back to producing theatre in 2007 and one of its shows is now one of the biggest local box office success stories of all time – Brick Up The Mersey Tunnels.

Around the corner in Williamson Square is the Liverpool Playhouse, which started life as a music hall in 1866. The Playhouse has seen some of the world's greatest actors perform there. The Redgrave Family, who now have a top-floor room named after them, were regulars there and 'Sirs' such as Anthony Hopkins and Michael Gambon remember their time with fondness.

Now splendidly billed alongside The Everyman as: "Two Great Theatres: One Creative Heart", both venues – under the inspired leadership of Gemma Bodinetz and Deborah Aydon, the enterprising pair behind the "In Conversation With" series of evenings at Liverpool Cathedral – have become beacons for talent in the city.

The Unity Theatre in Hope Place, near the Philharmonic Hall, has built up a loyal audience. It has an excellent record in encouraging and staging new writing. From pre-World War Two and onwards, it was a powerful and passionate voice in the wilderness.

The late, great Adrian Henri once said Liverpool outshines London because when venues are closing in the capital, new ones open in our city, along with new concepts and projects. The Actors' Studio – owned by Pauline Daniels – proves it, supporting new writing and acting.

Bravo! Shakespeare would be proud that Liverpool and live theatre thrives all these centuries on.

Peter Grant

CINEMA

LIVERPOOL'S original Odeon cinema, which opened in London Road in 1942, was the home of thousands of first dates, nights out for great mates and even some of the biggest gigs in Liverpool's history, including the Beatles.

The Fab Four famously played the stage area at the cinema on December 8, 1963 and the following year it hosted the northern premiere of the Beatles' first film A Hard Day's Night.

The year 2008 spelled the final curtain for the London Road venue though, when after 74 years of celluloid history the grand old Odeon closed its doors for the very last time. Now, the sequel plays out down the road at Odeon Liverpool ONE.

Just six months after opening, the brand new 14-screen venue had topped the half-a-million audience mark.On average, 70,000 customers come to the Odeon each month, and showbiz stars and film fans have enjoyed a host of exclusive charity premieres and screenings for the likes of Quantum of Solace, Nowhere Boy, Fifteen Minutes That Shook The World and Burlesque Undressed.

For a little bit extra, you can book a seat in The Gallery, a strictly over-18s area with an exclusive bar, as well as luxurious large seats and complimentary refreshments. All that and the best view in the house.

With the Foundation for Art and Creative Technology (or FACT, as it's known to its mates) on the other side of town, a perhaps more intimate venue which is enjoying equal success,

Liverpool is tremendously well served. Films shown in the Wood Street building are programmed by two organisations, FACT and Picturehouse. Much of the FACT film programme relates to the exhibitions that are shown within the galleries, and are chosen to enhance and extend the exhibition experience. FACT also features special screenings and one-off events so keep checking the website for updates.

The Picturehouse film programme includes mainstream blockbusters but independent, art-house and foreign-language films are also central to their profile. FACT also showcases the work of local filmmakers from Liverpool and the surrounding areas. Liverpool Film Night is an open submission screening opportunity that happens three times a year in FACT's main cinema spaces.

With regular Kids' Clubs and Big Scream! for parents with babies, the FACT film programme of events has something for everyone – check out the membership scheme too, which offers some great discounts.

Out of town, and Woolton Picture House offers a unique cinema experience. Hidden away in the heart of Woolton Village and steeped in history, the art-deco picture house has an illustrious history dating back to the 1920s and was reputedly a childhood haunt of John Lennon. As well as showing many of the latest releases, this cinema also holds a number of classic film nights. Throw in friendly staff and its no wonder this gem attracts film-goers from afar.

Vicky Andrews

LISTINGS

FACT
88 Wood Street
Liverpool L1 4DQ
0151 707 4464
www.fact.co.uk

ODEON LIVERPOOL ONE
14 Paradise Street
Liverpool L1 8JF
0871 2244 007
www.odeon.co.uk

OUT OF TOWN

CINEWORLD
Montrose Way
Edge Lane Retail Park
Liverpool L13 1EW
0871 200 2000
www.cineworld.co.uk

CROSBY PLAZA
13 Crosby Road North
Waterloo, Liverpool
L22 0LD
www.plazacinema.org.uk

WOOLTON PICTURE HOUSE
3 Mason Street, Woolton
Liverpool L25 5JH
0151 428 3737
www.wooltonpicturehouse.com

■ Robert Carlyle and Samuel L Jackson in The 51st State

Welcome to Merseywood!

ITS popularity among film and TV directors has led to Liverpool being given a brand new nickname – Merseywood.

With such big names as Robert Carlyle, Samuel L Jackson, Robert Downey Jr, Jude Law and Dominic West having filmed in the city, it's no surprise that Liverpool has well and truly secured its place on the world-wide movie map. It is Liverpool's famous buildings and architecture and its unique streets which have drawn film makers to the city since 1896.

When the cameras start rolling, Liverpool can be transformed into any time . . . any place.

■ **Harry Potter and the Deathly Hallows (2010)** Warner Bros paid Merseytravel £20,000 to film in the murky depths of the Mersey tunnel for four nights. The money was donated to Wirral children's hospice Claire House.

■ **Powder (2010)** Hope Street Hotel, Alma De Cuba and Korova were used for locations in Kevin Sampson's story about the music industry and fictional band The Grams.

■ **Nowhere Boy (2009)** Directed by Sam Taylor-Wood, Nowhere Boy quietly sets in motion the seismic shift in music brought about by a Liverpool teen called John Lennon. The £6m film was shot in Liverpool before the cast headed to London's Ealing studio – Lennon's teenage haunts include Woolton Picture House.

■ **Sherlock Holmes (2009)** Robert Downey Jr and Jude Law descended on a chilly Mersey to film a series of pivotal scenes at the Stanley and Clarence Docks. These included a thrilling sequence where Holmes, Watson and Sherlock's duplicitous love interest Irene (Rachel McAdams) run a fiery gauntlet of massive explosions as they hunt the evil Lord Blackwood.

■ **Alfie (2004)** Jude Law revived the role of Alfie Atkins in a film he describes as a "re-think" rather than a "re-make." Although much of the movie was shot in the Big Apple, Liverpool was also used as a central part. The former Halifax building in Brunswick Street was transformed into a New York oriental antiques shop.

■ The Hunt for Red October. Left, Nowhere Boy, Powder and stars of Sherlock Holmes, Robert Downey Jr and Jude Law

The 51st State (2001) Samuel L lackson's gangster movie was set entirely n Liverpool, including a particularly nemorable clubbing scene inside Nation.

The Parole Officer (2001) astle Street was used in this Steve Coogan icture.

In the Name of the Father (1993) fine example of Liverpool doubling as ondon, Belfast and Dublin, with Faulkner quare being used to represent a park in ondon and the terraced streets of Anfield s a double for Belfast. St George's Hall oubled up as the Old Bailey.

■ **The Hunt for Red October (1990)** False snow was poured on to Liverpool's Museum and Central Library to represent Moscow, in this Sean Connory blockbuster.

■ **Young Sherlock (1985)** Steven Spielberg was looking for suitable Victorian architecture to substitute for the lobby of the Houses of Parliament. The eventual choice was St George's Hall.

■ **Letter To Brezhnev (1985)** Director Chris Bernard's breathtaking, opening sequence of the Liverpool waterfront proved a popular moment for Liverpudlians everywhere.

COMEDY

GAME for a laugh? Then you've come to the right place.

Liverpool is undoubtedly the king of comedy and amongst its many glistening jewels is the mighty Rawhide Comedy Club at the Royal Court Theatre.

One of the city's best-loved comedy haunts, Rawhide is now in its 15th year and sits comfortably at home in the debonair Art Deco surroundings of the theatre's Downstairs Bar. Acts range from pant-wettingly funny local comics to a handful of top names and with an award-winning chef to boot, it's easy to see why punters flock back week after week. Shows run on Thursday (cheap night), Friday and Saturday, but be warned – Rawhide's good reputation precedes it and tickets often sell out well in advance.

Down at the docks, Comedy Central at Baby Blue Bar & Restaurant is another comic gem. Set in a rustic yet suitably stylish exposed-brick basement, the popular show on every Thursday, Friday and Saturday night boasts a consistently entertaining line-up of local and national comedians.

Tasty, if slightly pricey, meal deals are also available and thanks to its seductive waterside location and steady flow of pitchers (although I'm not quite sure about the spaceship-esque loos), Comedy Central attracts a heady-mix of the good, the glamorous and the slightly naughty, welcoming a generous helping of lively hen and stag dos.

If it's a more intimate setting you're after, however, head to Laughterhouse Comedy at The Slaughterhouse on Fenwick Street. One of Liverpool's oldes boozers, its unique atmosphere, cosy underground location, and fine ales guarantee a good night out and past acts to tread the boards include Dara O'Briai

Funny bones

THE Scouse sense of humour is so legendary that, along with a thick accent and a passion for football (whether red or blue), it forms the mould that all the city's sons – and daughters – are made in.

Ken Dodd is always serious when he talks about his beloved art form: "People often ask me two questions – who my favourite comics are and who inspires me.

"They are two very different things. I like to hear laughter. Anyone who makes people laugh is my favourite. Comedians are everywhere – no matter what city or origin. But Liverpool is special. It really is 'Mirthyside' and it has produced some legendary people."

Think of the A to Z of comedians – there's Ricky Tomlinson, Stan Boardman, Jimmy Tarbuck, Lily Savage, Les Dennis, Faith Brown, Pauline Daniels, Freddie Starr, Johnny Vegas, Sean Styles, Willie Miller and John Bishop. Merseyside deserves its accolade as Capital of Comedy.

(Mock the Week), Jason Manford (8 Out Of 10 Cats) and Alan Carr.

Also fighting for its place on Liverpool's comedy walk of fame is newcomer Laughterhouse at Lenny's. One of the latest contenders on the city's comic scene, this night lurks in the illict surroundings of Lenny's Bar And Smoke Grill, a New York prohibition-style bar and eatery on Sir Thomas Street. Every Friday and Saturday night offers top-notch comedy in the sleekest of surroundings.

So if you're hankering after getting your funny bone tickled (without a Ken Dodd tickling stick in sight) you can be sure Liverpool won't disappoint.

Sarah Hooley

LISTINGS

COMEDY CENTRAL
Baby Blue, Albert Dock
Liverpool L3 4AF
0151 702 5834
www.jicomedy.co.uk

LAUGHTERHOUSE AT LENNY'S
Lenny's Bar & Smoke Grill
7-11 Sir Thomas Street
Liverpool L1 6BW
0151 236 6546
www.thecapitalofcomedy.com

LAUGHTERHOUSE COMEDY
The Slaughter House
Fenwick Street
Liverpool L2 7LS
www.thecapitalofcomedy.com

LIVERPOOL COMEDY FESTIVAL
www.liverpoolcomedyfestival.com
10 great days of laughter held during May each year, in venues around the city.

RAWHIDE COMEDY CLUB
Royal Court Liverpool
Liverpool L1 1HL
0870 787 1866
www.rawhidecomedy.co.uk

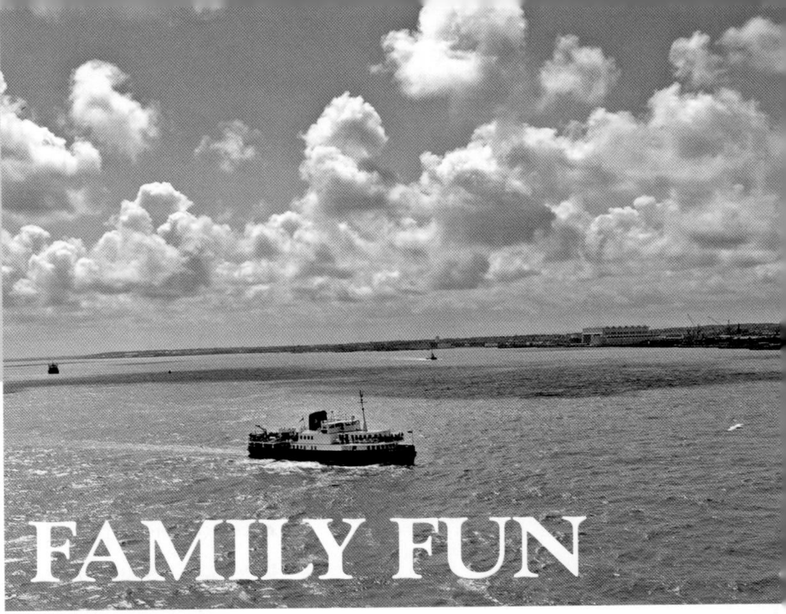

FAMILY FUN

WHETHER it's my secret penchant for Gerry and the Pacemakers or happy memories of Fred and his weather map – I've long had a love affair with Liverpool's historic waterfront.

So, it was with a rising feeling of shame that I found myself struggling to remember the last time I'd actually made the effort to really explore this part of the city. Six months ago? Two years?

Whatever the answer, it was most definitely too long, and it was on somewhat of a mission that I set off with my fiancé in tow to rediscover the city's waterscape.

An intrinsic part of the city's charm, Liverpool's waterfront has undergone an impressive makeover. And from the Albert Dock and ECHO Arena to the modern cruise liner facility and new-look Pier Head, the ever-changing waterfront is quite rightly one of the city's top attractions and pulls people in like shoppers at a half price sale in Primark.

So where to start? With so much to see and do we decided to embark on Mersey Ferries' Big Mersey Adventure and head to the new £10.5m Mersey Ferry terminal building at the Pier Head.

Tucked away behind the might of the Three Graces, the stylish Pier Head is awash with eager visitors and locals alike and after enjoying a quick snoop in the excellent gift shops we excitedly made our way to the Fab4D Experience.

One of the waterfront's newest attractions, Fab4D is a fantastic concoction of cutting edge 3D animation mixed together with a host of multi-sensory 'surprises' and a fantastic soundtrack of Beatles music – and judging by the audience's enthusiastic squeals of laughter, it's set to be a huge hit with kids and big kids alike.

Still giggling, we exited the auditorium and duly handed our 3D specs to the

Above, The Albert Dock
Right, Liverpool Ferry Terminal, fun in the sun and Fab4D

friendly host before making our way to the next stop on our hit list – the world famous Mersey Ferry. Making our way up to the top deck we find two empty seats facing Liverpool's enchanting skyline, and sit back and enjoy the ride.

Just 30 minutes later, the ferry docks at Seacombe and we head to Spaceport for an inspirational 'out of this world' journey through space. Previous special exhibitions at Spaceport have included the likes of Doctor Who, Alien Wars and Star Wars, so the Force is always strong with this one.

Back on planet Earth and we catch the short 10 minute ferry journey to our last stop, the U-boat Story at Woodside. A fantastic £5m attraction, the U-boat Story tells the mysterious tale of U-534, a German World War II submarine and inside we quickly delve into the museum's fantastic display of original artefacts and interactive exhibits.

However, it's the U-boat Story's spellbindingly eerie cross sections of the original U-534 that really wows, and with large viewing platforms for each part, the U-boat Story offers a unique insight into life under the sea.

Leaving the museum, we clamber on board the last of our ferries for the day and as we sink into our chairs we're already talking about returning to see more next weekend. After all, why should the tourists have all the fun?!

Sarah Hooley

CITY CENTRE

BIG ART FOR LITTLE ARTISTS

Walker Art Gallery
William Brown Street
Liverpool L3 8EL
0151 478 4199
www.liverpoolmuseums.org.uk

Inspire your child's creativity and introduce them to the amazing world of art at the Walker Art Gallery. Designed for children under eight, Big Art for Little Artists gives youngsters a chance to create their own art, dress up as characters from one of the Walker's paintings, listen to stories, play with puppets to create their own stories and much more besides.

THE BUGWORLD EXPERIENCE

The Grand Hall, Albert Dock
Liverpool L3 4AA
0151 708 4938
www.bugworldexperience.co.uk

Experience insects – see them, hold them and even eat them at the UK's first insectarium at the Albert Dock. Meet the Preying Mantis and the Salmon Pink Tarantula in Bugworld's simulated rainforest habitat, the Death Stalker Scorpion in the desert and in the woodland zone, the deadly Australian Redback Spider. At the Encounter Zone experience how a giant African millipede feels on your skin, handle a stick insect and listen to a hissing cockroach. At Base Camp taste yummy bugs such as leaf cutter ants and Mopani worms, and learn about bug recipes in everyday meals.

FAB4D

The Beatles Story
Pier Head, Liverpool L3
0151 709 1963
www.beatlesstory.com

An exciting multi-sensory 4D journey through the music of the Beatles. The 40-seat theatre, housed at the second Beatles Story site at the Mersey Ferries terminal, thrills audiences with a stunning 3D computer generated animation, combined with a dramatic 4th dimension – and a few surprises! Admission prices cover entry to both of The Beatles Story attractions.

SPACEPORT

Victoria Place, Seacombe
Wirral CH44 6QY
0151 330 1333
www.spaceport.org.uk

Blast off on a virtual journey though space and time at the amazing space-themed attraction at Seacombe Ferry Terminal on the Wirral. Explore space in the planetarium show in the space dome and experience the wondrous sights and sounds that an astronaut does in space in the 360 degree total immersion AV simulator. There are six galleries focusing on the solar system, the Milky Way and other aspects of space and space travel.

TATE LIVERPOOL

Albert Dock
Liverpool L3 4BB
0151 702 7400
www.tate.org.uk

Tate Liverpool's family room on the first floor of the gallery is a welcoming place for both kids and parents to relax and have fun with books, games, activity booklets and access to specially-designed online games. It also provides baby-changing facilities and can store buggies in the cloakroom.

UNDERWATER STREET

Cunard Building
Water Street, Pier Head
Liverpool L3 1DS
0151 227 2550
www.underwaterstreet.com

Discover a real 'hands-on' experience at Liverpool's

discovery centre for children. Divided into six fascinating zones, Underwater Street is a discovery centre with a difference. Construction, art and sensory areas, lab, physical zone and Imagination Village – highlights include panning for gold, painting a full-sized car and conducting interviews in a TV studio. Once you've worked up an appetite you can relax in the café, which serves a wide range of healthy food.

WOWBALLS
Duke's Dock, Liverpool and Marine Lake, New Brighton
0151 639 0466
www.wowballs.co.uk

Walk, run and skip on water without getting wet. Wowballs – walk-on-water inflatable balls – are totally enclosed two-metre high hamster spheres. Totally robust, you can run and skip in your Wowball and bash friends and family in theirs. You can hire them during weekends and school holidays, at Dukes Dock at the Albert Dock – between the Arena and the Albert Dock, and at the Marine Lake in New Brighton. They require calm weather so calling ahead first to ensure they are running is essential.

THE YELLOW DUCKMARINE
Gower Street, Albert Dock
Liverpool L3 4AS
0151 708 7799
www.theyellowduckmarine.co.uk

Kids will love a trip on The Yellow Duckmarine. Board the authentic World War II landing vehicle at the Albert Dock and enjoy an hour-long trip by road, taking in the historic waterfront, touring the famous sights of the city before making a dramatic splashdown in the Salthouse Dock. It's an amazing dockland adventure you'll never forget!

YELLOW SUB
Atlantic Way
Brunswick Business Park
Liverpool L3 4BE
08444 120 850
www.yellowsub.co.uk

A great way to tire the little ones out – this fantastic children's play centre boasts 14,000 sq ft of space crammed with slides and play frames guaranteed to keep even the most active kids occupied. The beauty of Yellow Sub is it appeals to children of all ages, from toddlers right up to those aged 12. In addition to the fabulous facilities on offer, there is also an award-winning restaurant serving everything from delicious breakfasts and freshly-made smoothies to healthy hot meals.

U-BOAT STORY
Woodside Ferry Terminal
Birkenhead CH41 6DU
0151 330 1000
www.u-boatstory.co.uk

Discover the amazing story of a German World War II U-534, through an interactive exhibition. A specially built viewing platform allows visitors to see inside, and alongside the U-Boat is one of the three T11 Zaukonig advanced homing torpedoes found on board – the most advanced torpedoes in the world at the end of the conflict. An adjoining centre contains artefacts from U-534, including an Enigma coding machine, interactive displays, filmed interviews with survivors, a pictorial history of life on board and personal effects of the crew including clothing and playing cards.

FURTHER AFIELD

ACORN FARM
Depot Road, Kirkby
Knowsley L33 3AR
0151 548 1524
www.acornfarm.co.uk

Beginning with just a rabbit and two gerbils, Acorn Farm has grown into an award-winning visitor attraction. It is now home to a wide range of farm animals including sheep, cattle, goats, pigs, horses, poultry rabbits and guinea pigs. Activities include petting small animals in the Petting Pavilion, including the opportunity to milk a goat, groom a rabbit and hold a chick. Acorn Farm was the winner of the Best Small Visitor Attraction 2009, in The Mersey Partnership Tourism Awards.

BLUE PLANET AQUARIUM
Kinsey Road CH65 9LF
0151 357 8804
www.blueplanetaquarium.com

Discover one of nature's most complex and stunning ecosystems at Blue Planet. Sharks, rays, starfish, clownfish and different types of coral will educate, amaze and enthuse you for the beauty of this natural world and the need to protect it. Reef Magic demonstrates the beauty and value of the 'nurseries' of the seas with a 2,000 litre freestanding tank so you can view 15 types of rainbow-coloured fish and 20 varieties of coral at 360 degrees. It also boasts one of the world's longest aqua tunnels, where you can get close to the aquarium's five varieties of shark.

CHESTER ZOO
Upton-by-Chester
Chester CH2 1EU
01244 380280
www.chesterzoo.org

The UK's number one zoo attracts more than 1million visitors every year and it's not hard to understand why. It is home to more than 7000 animals and 400 species, including many of the most endangered on the planet. Highlights include the Realm of the Red Ape, an Indonesian forest-themed exhibit that immerses visitors in the world of the forest canopy and its teeming biodiversity. Marvel at the elephants of the Asian forest, wander through the tropical house and bat zone or monorail it above the Black Rhinos, big cats and spectacled bears.

CHURCH FARM
Church Lane, Thurstaston
Wirral CH61 0HW
0151 648 7838
www.churchfarm.org.uk

A 60-acre organic farm with a wide variety of farm animals and crops. Livestock includes pigs, cows, sheep, hens, rabbits and alpacas. The farm runs special seasonal events, tractor tours and a lavender maze.

CROXTETH HOME FARM
Croxteth Hall Lane
Liverpool L12 0HB
0151 233 6910
www.croxteth.co.uk

The heady mix of an Edwardian stately home, a Victorian walled garden and a rare breeds farm has drawn visitors from far and wide, making this country park one of Merseyside's top 10 tourist attractions. Children and adults will enjoy the sights and sounds of country life at Home Farm. Get close to all the animals – cows, pigs, horses and sheep – on a real working farm.

GULLIVER'S THEME PARK
Warrington WA5 9YZ
(M62 junction 8/9)
01925 444888
www.gulliversfun.co.uk

Spend the whole day spinning around, turning upside-down and flying through the air, at Gulliver's. This theme park is brilliant for younger visitors. It is, in essence, a junior theme park, giving excitement and fun without the stomach-churning adrenalin rush of the adult-based attractions. Adults can go on many of the rides with them – which adds to the feel of a family day out. Watch out for special seasonal events and bring a picnic.

KNOWSLEY SAFARI PARK

Prescot,
Merseyside L34 4AN
0151 430 9009
www.knowsleysafariexperience.co.uk

There's more to Knowsley Safari Park than baboons. But baboons and indeed all the apes remain some of the most popular inhabitants of this famous drive-through attraction. Knowsley is also the place to view some of the world's rather larger, fiercer wildlife. There are African elephants, lions, tigers, endangered white rhinoceroses, ostriches and emus. The sea-lion show is particularly popular with younger children.

MARTIN MERE WILDFOWL AND WETLANDS TRUST

Fish Lane, Burscough
Ormskirk L40 0TA
01704 895181
www.wwt.org.uk

Home to over 100 species of rare and endangered ducks, geese, swans, flamingos and beavers. Hand feed the birds and look out for the baby goslings and ducklings as they start springing up.

NATIONAL WILDFLOWER CENTRE

Court Hey Park, Roby Road
Liverpool L16 3NA
0151 738 1913
www.nwc.org.uk

The award-winning National Wildflower Centre is a family-friendly visitor centre and conference venue dedicated to promoting new wildflower environments for people and wildlife to enjoy. The centre is set in the 35-acre Victorian Court Hey Park in Knowsley, and offers wildflower demonstration areas, a working garden nursery, children's play area, a shop, a cafe and loads of information about wildflowers. A fantastic place to start getting children interested in the environment.

NESS BOTANIC GARDENS

Ness, Neston
South Wirral CH64 4AY
0151 353 0123
www.nessgardens.org.uk

Forty-six acres of ornamental gardens featuring woods, herbaceous borders, rhododendrons, terraces, rockeries, herbs, glass houses and a laburnum arch. The visitor centre, with its roof of growing sedum and exhibition area, incorporates gift and plant shops and a cafe.

NEW PALACE & ADVENTURELAND

Marine Promenade
New Brighton CH45 2JX
0151 639 6041
www.wlgltd.co.uk

Family fun-filled entertainment whatever the weather, with indoor and outdoor activities. Suitable for toddlers to age 13, Adventureland is one of the largest indoor children's play areas in the country and includes a 30ft snake slide, a 25ft climbing wall, ropes, ball ponds, large inflatables and soft play areas. The outdoor fairground features dodgems and a fun house while the family arcade has everything from 2p plays to dance simulators. The Wirral Line station in New Brighton is just a five-minute walk.

RICE LANE CITY FARM

Walton Park Cemetary
Walton L9 1AW
0151 530 1066
www.ricelanecityfarm.co.uk

Keep the little ones happy at Rice Lane City Farm, set in countryside and woodland by Walton Park Cemetary. Just ten minutes' walk from Walton rail station on the Northern Line, the farm has a variety of farm animals including pigs, cattle, award-winning sheep as well as goats, rabbits and geese.

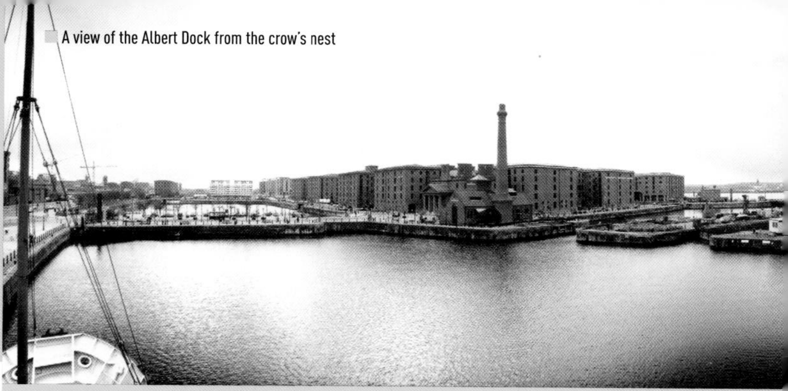

A view of the Albert Dock from the crow's nest

A Royal jewel for all seasons

"I HAVE heard of the greatness of Liverpool but the reality far surpasses the expectation," proclaimed Prince Albert on opening the Albert Dock on July 30 1846.

Today there's still a sense of greatness about the buildings, not just in the architectural achievement, but in the fact that the dock, like its mother city, has triumphed over adversity – from the Blitz through prolonged neglect and recession – to stand steadfast in the midst of an accelerating environment.

While so much of the surrounding city has fast become a modern metropolis with shining steel, granite and glass, the dock warehouses retain a fortified elegance. Purpose-built to accommodate sailing ships with up to 1000 tons' cargo capacity, the water is home to an increasing array of historic ships and modern pleasure boats, while the dock buildings now host a variety of shops, attractions, cafes, restaurants, bars and hotels.

Versatility has been the key to the dock's survival – in the ongoing epic movie that is Liverpool's resurgence, it has set many a scene from Gothic Horrors, Dickensian Christmases, Pirate Battles, remembered Beatles and held red carpet, crowd-wowing celebrity events such as This Morning television series and the MTV Awards.

And then there's the boats and races, from the Tall Ships and Round The World Clipper to the Powerboat, Yacht and Dragon Boats. The dock can adapt with the tide and greets each turn of fortune with resilience.

So what will today's visitor discover?

Like many modern attractions, it is best to leave the motor at home, but if you can't, there is a multi-storey car park at the neighbouring King's Dock (by the Arena) that is well managed and has a reasonable charge. There is also an excellent circular bus service, which picks up throughout the city centre and sets you down inside the dock estate.

It is definitely worth setting aside at least a half-day to take in all the attractions. Here you will find one of two impressive Beatles Story exhibitions, Tate Liverpool, the award-winning International Museum of Slavery and the Merseyside Maritime Museum, which also houses the National Merchant Navy Museum. The museums are free, as are many exhibitions at the Tate.

The plan of the dock resembles a board game or giant jigsaw piece, around which are sited the shops, bars, cafes and restaurants.

Shiver me timbers! Pirate day at the Albert Dock

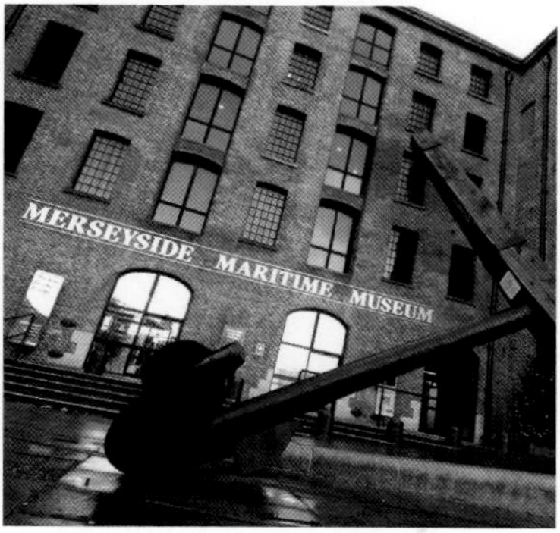

n keeping with the boats, life passes at a slower pace here during the day. At night, the lights from the bars twinkle across the dock as the river rocks to the rhythm of the night's revellers.

All the restaurants and cafes face the water, and you can choose from menus as varied as the cargos that once were hauled into the warehouses, with Italian, Indian, American, continental bistros and cosmopolitan cafes.

There are the expected souvenir shops, but there are some different and quirky treasures to unearth, from the Maritime Traditionalist Emporium Nauticalia to Liverpool Impressions. Art is on offer, not just at the Tate, but in vintage prints at Liverpool Pictures to the contemporary and stylish Freshwater Gallery.

The water from the river is what lends magic to this austere site, with the ever present breeze to blow away the cobwebs.

Prince Albert knew what he was talking about . . .

Peter Grant

Snap happy

■ Spring in Liverpo
as daffodils bloo

LIVERPOOL Daily Post and ECHO picture editor, Stephen Shakeshaft, is an award-winning photographer who has spent the last four decades chronicling the city.

From soccer stars to super stars, Stephen's work has been exhibited in prestigious venues across Liverpool, and earned him a privileged place in the UK Press Gazette's Hall of Fame for his life-long contribution to photography.

So, when it comes to taking snap shots of Liverpool, who better to ask than the man himself?

"When you're travelling to any city, buy six well-taken postcards that you can put together with your own pictures." Stephen suggests. "The most interesting pictures always have friends and family on them, so the postcards will give you the basic shot, while your pictures add a personal perspective.

"Also, the light tends to be better for photographs during early morning or sunset, and you'll find attractions won't be as busy during these times.

"Try and keep away from the obvious, but bear in mind that the same location can produce many different pictures depending on the photographer.

"Then there's the basics. Try to keep the camera still, and frame your picture. Also, take a number of pictures, thanks to digital cameras you can take and discard as many as you like, so don't be mean with your shutter."

Tall Ships on the River Mersey

Architecture from three centuries

Working out on the causeway, West Kirby

A colourful scene outside an antiques shop in Seel Street

Here are Stephen's tips on where to head to find the best photo opportunities in the city:

The Liverpool Waterfront

"You will get the most spectacular view of the Liverpool waterfront by taking a ferry. Also, any picture taken from the ferry will give you the most up-to-date scene of Liverpool. Alternatively, the waterfront looks spectacular at night, so it's well worth taking a trip across the Mersey to Seacombe as the sun sets. Liverpool looks so dramatic around that time, like a mini Manhattan."

Everton Heights

"If you would like to avoid the traditional tourist route, take a taxi to Netherfield Road. At Everton Heights, you'll find a jewel that most tourists don't get to see."

Albert Dock

"This is a popular location for tourists, but if you ask your subject to stand outside the Tate gallery, you will find you get the Anglican Cathedral framing the shot."

King's Dock

"Ask your subject to stand in the foreground of the new stadium. This will make for quite a dramatic shot, especially as the new stadium has that sense of a huge ship docking in the background."

Crosby Beach

"Take a visit to Crosby Beach where you can take some really fun pictures with the Antony Gormley statues. These allow for lots of interfacing between the subject, and give a topical shot of Liverpool."

St John's Gardens and William Brown Street

"This is a lovely area, especially as night falls – at sunset it just looks spectacular. Try to take a shot in that light as the buildings look extraordinary and the photograph can be nicely framed by the trees in the gardens."

St George's Plateau

"This is a great location wherever you photograph it from. You've got the steps and collonades if you stand across the way on Lime Street. Plus the lions look striking in the foreground."

Country life in the city

VISITORS to Liverpool are often surprised by the open squares and spacious streets in the heart of the city – by the breadth and openness of our waterfront and by the broad avenues and boulevards that radiate from the city centre into the extensive suburbs.

Liverpool's distinctive collection of parks is all thanks to the foresight of the city's great Victorian civic leaders, who battled to keep at least part of Liverpool as a green and pleasant land amid the rapid industrialisation of the country.

Sefton Park, Calderstones Park, Newsham Park and Princes Park represent those legacies from the 19th century.

It is a remarkable fact that Liverpool's parks and open spaces now cover approximately 3,000 acres, or one-ninth of the City's land area. These true, green open spaces are very diverse – Liverpool has pretty much an example of every kind of park created in the past 200 years.

Sefton Park is probably the most celebrated of our open spaces – civic planners across the world have long admired the fine example of imaginative design which was created by French landscaper Edouard Andre and Liverpool architect Lewis Hornblower and opened by Queen Victoria's son, Prince Arthur, on May 20 1872.

The 69-acre Princes Park, opened in 1842, was laid out by Joseph Paxton, who would later win even greater fame for Birkenhead Park (1847) and the Crystal Palace (1851).

Sefton Park in autumn

In 1850 American Frederick Olmsted visited Birkenhead Park as part of a tour of Europe. He later became famous as the designer of New York's Central Park, into which he incorporated many of the features he first observed in its little-known predecessor in the Wirral town. Birkenhead Park is recognised as the oldest public-funded park in the world. Today, the lakes form a major feature of the park that also boasts a spectacular Swiss Bridge and Boathouse.

Calderstones Park is home to the 4,000-year-old, 5-ft high Calder Stones after which the park and surrounding area was named. Mystery surrounds these ancient carved sandstones, which were discovered in 1550 but date back to the Bronze Age, making them older than Stonehenge. A more recent addition to the park, which is also home to the 1,000-year-old Allerton Oak tree, is the children's playground, opened by Sir Paul McCartney in 2000 and dedicated to his late wife, Linda.

Calderstones Park

Other features at Calderstones include the unique plant collection, specialist gardens and lake, Georgian-style Mansion House and the Stable Block, Coach House and Lancastrian Barn which play host to regular arts and crafts exhibitions. If ever there was a hidden gem among Liverpool's suburbs then Calderstones Park is it.

Princes Park is sandwiched between Sefton

Victorian Day at the Isla Gladstone Conservatory in Stanley Park

Park and Princes Road, while Newsham Park offers a huge "green lung" in the heart of a heavily built-up area of the city.

A multi-million pound scheme has transformed the Gladstone Conservatory, in Anfield's Stanley Park. The £12m restoration project required the expertise of specialists from all over the country to make the space – disused for 30 years – a lush, period-style inner-city haven.

Flying a kite along Otterspool Prom, competing with the other parents to send it highest in the sky while enjoying a view of the River Mersey, is a unique Liverpool experience. The prom stretches from the Britannia Inn on Riverside Drive for several miles towards Grassendale and close by is one of Liverpool's hidden gems, Otterspool Park, that cuts through a tree-lined ravine.

For an oasis of calm in the city centre, St John's Ornamental and Memorial Garden behind St George's Hall is well worth investigating. The garden contains a number of statues and memorials to local people, as well as commemorative trees planted to remember John Lennon and George Harrison – a favourite place for visitors to the World Museum to gather and picnic.

A walk in the park is one of the greatest free pleasures in life and in Merseyside we are blessed with wonderful green spaces, in pleasant and fascinating settings, that are just waiting to be discovered.

Dance among the palms

LIVERPOOL'S Grade II-listed Sefton Park is a beautiful green haven and one of the best parks in the world.

Restoration work on the Victorian park will be completed in the summer of 2010, marking the culmination of a £6m, three-year project.

The wide-ranging makeover of Sefton Park has seen repairs to the banks of the boating lake, restoration work on the monuments and fountains and a new lakeside refreshment kiosk, created on the site of the former boathouse.

The works also included the clearing away of overgrowth from watercourses to reveal previously hidden treasures, such as waterfalls and a small island by the William Rathbone monument.

Signposting, seating and pathways have also been improved, along with the creation of a new children's play area. The famous bandstand – said to have been the inspiration for Sgt Pepper's Lonely Hearts Club Band – was fully renovated by specialists and is now back in its original home near the lake.

Park visitors will have the use of a refreshment kiosk and it is hoped that boats will be available for hire on the lake. The Shaftesbury memorial fountain has a fully restored bronze base and a replica of its famous Eros statue.

The Greek god of love – now made of more weatherproof material – stands still on his feet pointing at passers-by with his arrows, ready to spread his contagious feelings of ardour.

Sefton Park Palm House's fine glass and great dome, like a billowing glass crinoline, was superbly restored in 2001 by a dedicated team of local residents.

For years this 1896 child of Kew and the Crystal Palace lay derelict, but is now a splendid functions venue – keep an eye out for public events including concerts, children's activities and the monthly Tea Dance Amidst the Palms.

FUN FOR FREE

St George's Hall Heritage Centre
Since completion of a £23 million restoration, St George's Hall has been open to the public as one of Liverpool's most fascinating heritage centres and gallery spaces.

Formby Point Squirrel Reserve
Formby Point boasts not only distinctive sand dunes but glorious pine woods, home to endangered red squirrels – catch them while you can.

World Museum Liverpool
Featuring historic treasures from across the globe with the latest interactive technology – an amazing day out for young and old.

Chinatown
Built around a cluster of Chinese restaurants, Liverpool's Chinatown is home to one of the largest Chinese communities in Europe. Check out the amazing Chinese Arch, shops and Sunday market.

Anthony Gormley's Another Place
One hundred iron statues situated on Crosby beach. Don't be afraid to be creative with them in the name of a good photo opportunity.

Hope Street
Take in the twilight magnificence of Liverpool's two cathedrals on an evening stroll down Hope Street. With plenty of bars and restaurants along the way, it's the perfect way to admire these two stunning icons of the city skyline.

Sefton Park
When the sun is shining, there is no better place to be than the "Hyde Park of the North". Look out for the stunning Palm House as well as the Shaftesbury Memorial and Eros Fountain, Fairy Glen, bandstand and boating lake.

The Albert Dock
The dock has everything a blurry-being needs to start the day – fresh air, scenery and a walk for good measure.

MUSIC

WIND your way down a Liverpool street and it won't take long before you hear the tell-tale sounds of live music drifting towards your ears.

Everyone knows the live music scene is good in the city. It always has been. It's probably always going to be true that if you throw a stone in Liverpool you'll hit a performer or entertainer of some kind.

There's a good grouping of very worthy venues at the fringes of Liverpool's Ropewalks area of the city. It's a useful crossover space where the popular city nightlife spots meet the student bars. The Zanzibar on Seel Street is a local mecca for music – every band worth their amps has rocked it, including some famous names.

Also on Seel Street you'll find The Masque venue. Chances are there'll be something happening here – anything from acoustic acts to local DJs or an up-and-coming young band playing a showcase for their new album. Nearby you could see those trying their hand at an open mic night at The Jacaranda (Slater St) or Pogue Mahone's (Seel St). Check the Metropolitan (Berry St) or Heebie Jeebies (Seel St) for an impromptu live set or some laid back sounds at Parr Street's 3345 – you never know, you might even spot a Zuton or two in there.

One look around Korova shows that everyone there is in a band. Some are working there, others drinking. There's normally a singer or two behind the bar, and a drummer supervising a delivery outside. Obviously there's loads more places around the city, but exploring this concentrated area will offer you both choice and quality for your live music buck.

Paul Baker

LISTINGS

LIVE LOUNGE @ BABY BLUE
Albert Dock
Liverpool L3 4AB
0844 8000 400
www.blue-venue.co.uk
An intimate night of live music in stylish surroundings.

BADFORMAT SOCIAL CLUB
3-5 Trueman Street
Liverpool L3 2BA
0151 227 5388
www.badformat.com
One of the city's newer venues – puts on some great live shows, DJs and cabaret.

BUMPER
18 Hardman Street
Liverpool L1 9AX
0151 707 9902
www.bumperliverpool.co.uk
A live favourite, backed up with a nomination from the Great British Pub Awards.

ECHO ARENA LIVERPOOL
Monarch's Quay
Liverpool L3 4FP
0844 8000 400
www.echoarena.com
The place to catch all your favourite megastars such as Beyonce, Rhianna, Elton John, Kings of Leon and Girls Aloud– the true measure of this venue's success is that it's difficult to remember it not being there.

THE KAZIMIER
Wolstenholme Square
Liverpool L1 4JJ
www.thekazimier.co.uk
A rich and diverse venue with underground roots and a low profile.

Bicycle Thieves at The Masque
Picture: Sakura

KOROVA
32 Hope Street
Liverpool L1 9BX
0151 709 7097
www.korova-liverpool.com
With a clientele that reads like a who's who of Liverpool's music scene, Korova is the uber-cool king of the indie glitterati. We all know by now of the impressive music credentials and Korova's ability to spot up-and-coming talent a mile off. So all club nights and gigs can potentially mean you'll be witnessing something special.

THE MAGNET
45 Hardman Street
Liverpool L1 9AS
0151 709 7560
www.magnetliverpool.co.uk
The Emile Heskey of Liverpool venues – it doesn't put on a good gig for a while, but when it does, it's an absolute whopper. Down the stairs and into the funky area in front of the stage will do us. Great sound, too.

THE MASQUE
90 Seel Street
Liverpool L1 4BH
0151 707 6171
www.masque-liverpool.com

Born out of the ashes of the old Barfly, The Masque offers a diverse line-up of bands as well as showcases for unsigned local talent. The original venue boasted a stage in the main room, which thankfully remains, as does the dancefloor/mosh pit, which has been bouncing since the relaunch in 2009.

FREE ROCK & ROLL @ MELLO MELLO
40-42 Slater Street
Liverpool L1 4BX
www.myspace.com/freerockandroll

Pete Bentham (of local punk-rock heroes Pete Bentham and the Dinner Ladies) has been dishing out gigs to those hungry for something other than corporate venues for some time now. Currently residing at Mello Mello every other Thursday, Free Rock & Roll is sweaty, noisy and always enjoyable, with an eclectic sort of crowd. And all for free!

MOUNTFORD HALL
160 Mount Pleasant
Liverpool L69 7BR
0151 794 6868
www.lgos.org

Mountford Hall used to be the place to see live music in Liverpool, where all the big touring acts stopped off. It's still an amazing venue with great sound and atmosphere – just very underused these days.

THE NEW PICKET
61 Jordan Street
Liverpool L1 0BW
0151 708 6789
www.mypsace.com/picketliverpool

One of Liverpool's most famous music venues, thriving in its new home within the Baltic Triangle creative quarter.

O2 ACADEMY LIVERPOOL
11-13 Hotham Street
Liverpool L3 5UF
0151 707 3200
www.o2academyliverpool.co.uk

A hot spot for alternative and dance acts visiting in the city, from Arctic Monkeys to Dizzee Rascal, taking in Hot Chip, Blondie and Queens of The Stone Age along the way. On the downside, drinks prices are anything but music to your ears.

OLYMPIA
West Derby Road
Liverpool L6 9BY
0151 263 6633
www.liverpoololympia.com

The ballroom was originally known as Locarno, and has been a key venue in the city for over 70 years. The Olympia now hosts a diverse range of events, ranging from boxing to blasts from the past courtesy of The Grafton, but memorable gigs have included The Specials and Echo & the Bunnymen.

PACIFIC ROAD ARTS CENTRE
Pacific Road
Birkenhead CH41 1LJ
0151 666 0000
www.pacificroad.co.uk

Always worth crossing the river for, especially when they have an artist on who needs that little bit of intimacy to get something special going. Hosts a regular programme of events with an emphasis on music and one-man shows, including jazz, classical, folk and pop. Pacific Road works best as a sit-down gig venue and a place where people can listen to a picked acoustic guitar note or a joyous, acapella vocal.

THE PHILHARMONIC HALL
Hope Street
Liverpool
0151 709 3789
www.liverpoolphil.com

One of the UK's top arts and entertainment venues and home of the Royal Liverpool Philharmonic Orchestra. There's a year-round programme with top names from classical (pictured is Simon Rattle), contemporary and chamber music, folk, roots, jazz, blues, rock, pop, comedy and spoken word. Van Morrison, Christy Moore, Joan Armatrading and Chris Rea have all got the old hall going in recent years. Morrissey too, had a great night on Hope Street.
The big stage lends itself well to more eclectic styles, like that of The Bays Orchestra and African Soul Rebels. And you won't find better acoustics in the city.
Upstairs, the intimate Rodewald Suite is the place to see some of your favourite roots and jazz artists unplugged. Small, but perfectly formed, this place is an unsung gem.

ROCKSCAPE
95-99 Renshaw Street
Liverpool L1 2SP

Open-air theatre at the bottom of Leece Street, designed by Japanese architects Atelier Bow-Wow, in the form of a traditional Greek amphitheatre. Keep your eyes peeled during the summer months for local bands performing here.

ST BRIDE'S CHURCH
Percy Street
Liverpool L8 7LT
www.stbridesliverpool.com

Could be the best-kept secret of Liverpool live music venues – a creative, progressive and inclusive church which has opened its doors to Liverpool's musical community, converting itself into a rehearsal space, recording studio and live music venue.

STUDIO 2
33-45 Parr Street
Liverpool L1 4JN
0151 707 3727
www.parrstreet.co.uk

Studio 2 hosts relaxed acoustic gigs throughout the week, including ParrJazz every Tuesday. There is no loud music, sticky dancefloor or burly doorman. Just good music and good times.

VIEW TWO
23 Mathew Street
Liverpool L2 6RE
0151 236 9444
www.viewtwogallery.co.uk

An island of calm above the bustling crowds of Mathew Street, View Two is a great place to hear our more delicate acts and artists.

THE ZANZIBAR
43 Seel Street
Liverpool L1 4AZ
0151 707 0633
www.thezanzibarclub.com

It doesn't matter if The Zanzi is hosting indie superstars or bouncing with the sounds of local heroes, the atmosphere in the place can be electric.

St Bride's Church

THE BEATLES

THEY are bigger and as popular now as in their hey day.

The Beatles may have split up in 1970 after eight years at the toppermost of the poppermost – but their fab legacy lives on. When they went their separate ways their own hometown did not respond to their enormous potential as a visitor attraction. But in 1983 teacher Bill Heckle and taxi driver Dave Jones saw just what we had in the city – Beatle-wise – and created Cavern City Tours. It has gone from strength to strength.

They came up with the Mathew Street Festival, which takes place on August Bank Holiday weekend every year – the culmination to International Beatle Week – and they are the people behind the must-do Magical Mystery Tours that take fans away on a real star trek in a replica of the multi-coloured psychedelic coach depicted in the 1967 TV film.

It can be seen coasting around the city – sometimes eight days a week – well, anything is possible in Beatleland. On this one hour 45 minute journey you can see where John, Paul, George and Ringo spent their childhoods and the places that inspired them such as Penny Lane and Strawberry Fields.

Beatle expert guides fill you in on the Fabbest story ever told. The tour finishes at the recreated Cavern Club, the legendary venue where the four lads who shook the world played nearly 300 times.

It was Bill and Dave who also came up

with the initial concept for the superb Hard Days Night Hotel in 1995. In March 2010 this 110-bedroomed Liverpool boutique hotel, inspired by the Beatles, celebrated its second birthday. It is Four Stars – does it sound familiar?

Another Fab thing to do in Liverpool is the National Trust mini-bus tours to the childhood homes of Paul McCartney and John Lennon. The National Trust looks after two suburban houses – Number 20 Forthlin Road (Paul's) and Mendips (John's). Anyone visiting these houses will find it an unforgettable experience, places you will remember all your life where the most famous songwriting partnership of the 20th century wrote some of the timeless Beatles classics. A splendid time is guaranteed for all.

West Derby is a key location for Beatles fans. The Casbah is the only original Beatles venue to remain untouched and is the first place they played as the Quarrymen in the basement of this wonderful Victorian house, opened in 1959 by Mona Best – the mother of original Beatles' drummer Pete.

And no one should leave Liverpool without seeing The Beatles Story, which has tripled in size and is now on two sites at the Albert Dock and Pier Head.

It is an award-winning exhibition that will have you smiling with delight and moved in equal measure when you see the finest collection of Moptop Memorabilia, lovingly put together to do the Beatles and the city proud.

It is an astonishing tribute to their lives, times and culture with breathtaking interactive displays.

Oh and don't forget, one thing is compulsory after you have seen all these super sites – go home and play the music to see and hear what the fuss was about!

Peter Grant

LISTINGS

THE BEATLES STORY

Albert Dock
Liverpool L3 4AD
0151 709 1963
www.beatlesstory.com

The full story of the Beatles' genesis, rise to fame and lasting musical legacy, exploring their sojourn in West Germany, Cavern Club gigs and psychedelic era along the way.

FAB FOUR TAXI TOUR

www.thebeatlesfabfourtaxitour.co.uk

Five people fit into these black cabs, so grab some friends. Visit Penny Lane, Strawberry Fields, Mathew Street and much more. Find out about the places that played an important part in the story of the Beatles, like where John and Paul met or where John and Cynthia got married, and all about the people themselves. The taxi tours operate with drivers all trained carefully in Beatles folklore, and takes in the history of the city as well.

MAGICAL MYSTERY TOUR

Cavern City Tours
www.cavernclub.org

The Magical Mystery Tour is a must for anyone of any age who enjoys music – and it's the perfect way to discover the city of The Beatles. Step aboard the colourful bus for this one hour 45 minute tour visiting many of the places associated with John, Paul, George and Ringo as they grew up, met and formed the band that would take the pop world by storm. Make sure you bring your camera to record the places you'll want to remember on this magical tour. You'll be kept entertained by one of the fully qualified Beatles Guides as you travel around the city and its suburbs to discover the truly remarkable story of the boys who were to become the world's best-known musicians. The tour finishes at the legendary Cavern Club where you can present your ticket for an exclusive souvenir of your trip.

NATIONAL TRUST – THE BEATLES' CHILDHOOD HOMES
www.nationaltrust.org.uk
The National Trust looks after two suburban houses in Merseyside at 20 Forthlin Road and Mendips. These unassuming houses are the childhood homes of two Beatles, Sir Paul McCartney and John Lennon. Mendips was the house where John Lennon lived with his aunt during his youth and wrote early songs. Highlights include Lennon's bedroom, audio interviews with former student lodgers, photographs and memorabilia. Number 20 Forthlin Road in Allerton was the childhood home of Sir Paul McCartney, where the Beatles rehearsed and wrote songs. Visiting the Beatles' houses in Liverpool is an absolute must for fans of the band of any age. The tours provide a real insight into Lennon and McCartney's humble beginnings. Beatles tours are available from February to November, and get booked up quickly.

The Casbah

INTERNATIONAL BEATLE WEEK FESTIVAL
http://beatlesfestival.co.uk/
Organised by Cavern City Tours, the International Beatle Week Festival takes place in late August and is one of the biggest music events in the world. And it is in the city where it all began – Liverpool. There is so much to do and see that you do not need to be a Beatles fan to enjoy the festival, though it helps! This is truly an international event with bands from over 20 countries and fans from over 40. As well as live gigs, there are exhibitions, memorabilia sales, guest speakers, video shows, sightseeing tours and a convention.

THE CASBAH COFFEE CLUB
8 Haymans Green
West Derby
Liverpool L12 7JG
0151 280 3519
Awarded Grade II listed status by English Heritage because of its international importance in the "popular cultural phenomenon" that was the Beatles. The band signed their first contract with manager Brian Epstein here. The Casbah closed in 1962 with a Beatles concert on the

final night in front of 1500 people, and has remained unaltered, now a popular tourist attraction. The basement still contains murals and paintings by John, George, Paul and Pete Best.

THE JACARANDA
21-23 Slater Street
Liverpool L1 4BW

The Jacaranda was founded by Allan Williams, the Beatles' first manager and "the man who gave them away". The Fab Four once played here and original art work remains from Beatles' fifth member, Stuart Sutcliffe. The walls are filled with pictures of the Beatles as well as Cilla Black and Brian Epstein, alongside posters for seemingly every Beatles-related movie, play and revue. Nestled among them is the celebrated 1956 school picture of pupils at the Liverpool Institute, in which can be seen Paul and Mike McCartney, George Harrison, Peter Sissons and various members of Gerry and The Pacemakers, Remo Four and the Quarrymen.

ELEANOR RIGBY STATUE
Stanley Street
Liverpool L1 6AL

One of Liverpool's most popular photo opportunities, a bronze statue sculptured by the 1950s song and dance man Tommy Steele, famous for the film Half A Sixpence. It is dedicated to 'All the Lonely People', according to the sign. Tommy accepted half a sixpence for the commission but it's worth its weight in gold, tourism wise. Inside the cavity of the statue is a Liverpool Echo, a pair of football boots . . . and the other half of that sixpence!

THE BEATLES SHOP
31 Mathew Street
Liverpool L2 6RE
www.thebeatlesshop.co.uk

Fascinating little shop, devoted entirely to the Beatles. Manager Steven Bailey also looks after the annual Beatle auction. The array of items is truly fab and there are new additions all the time. Visitors to the shop have included Ringo Starr, who was in Liverpool making a film about his childhood.

Sir George Martin popped in and so, too, did George Harrison. Next door is the Mathew Street Gallery, which has gained a reputation for presenting excellent Beatles-associated art and photographic exhibitions.

PENNY LANE
L18

Most of the things mentioned in the Beatles' song are still there: the barbers, the bank, the fire station – well worth a visit for a taste of Liverpool as the Beatles knew it. The street owes its name to James Penny, an 18th century Liverpool merchant who made his money from the transportation of slaves. To get there, take the Arriva 86 bus from the city.

FESTIVALS

The Brouhaha Carnival

AFRICA OYÉ

www.africaoye.com

Africa Oyé is a unique and inspiring free festival that offers great entertainment and fun, and some of the best culture this city has to offer. Thousands flock to Sefton Park for the two-day celebration, which offers a wide range of world music, as well as more than 40 stalls selling food, drink, arts, crafts and fashion from Africa and beyond. The crowd is multi-age, multi-ethnic and multi-background, which adds to the festival atmosphere. Bring a picnic and an umbrella – the festival was famously washed out in 2005 just minutes after a band performed a rain dance! But Africa always manages to sizzle through the English drizzle, and rain or shine, it is a fantastic couple of days.

BROUHAHA INTERNATIONAL STREET FESTIVAL

www.brouhaha.uk.com

Carnival fever comes to Liverpool every summer at the Brouhaha International Street Festival, when more than 300 performers from five continents join together to celebrate our culturally-diverse landscape. Music concerts and jam sessions take place all over Liverpool during July and August, with many events held outside the city centre to involve all of our communities. The highlight of the Brouhaha festival is the Saturday carnival, which winds its way through the streets of Toxteth as thousands cheer the performers in an array of spectacular costumes. The giant street party continues as musicians and dancers from all over the world perform at stages in Princes Park.

CREAMFIELDS

www.creamfields.com

More than 60,000 music fans and party animals descend on the sleepy Cheshire village of Daresbury during August Bank Holiday for the world's best dance music festival. The two-day Creamfields extravaganza, which moved from Liverpool's former airfield at Speke in 2006, sees live performances from top DJs and dance acts that have included Tiësto, Paul van Dyk, Judge Jules, Basement Jaxx, Chemical Brothers and Calvin Harris. Standard weekend tickets with camping, hospitality weekend tickets and day tickets are available.

INTERNATIONAL GUITAR FESTIVAL OF GREAT BRITAIN

www.bestguitarfest.com

November is the month of the guitar in Wirral! The borough's International Guitar Festival features concerts by some of the world's top classical, jazz, blues, folk and rock players. The programme includes the breathtaking wizardry of virtuoso players who will dazzle the most demanding critic, in a series of events that deliver the most enjoyable musical experience to those looking for a good time and good company, as well as those technical aficionados.

LIVERPOOL IRISH FESTIVAL

www.liverpoolirishfestival.com

A celebration of the strong cultural links between Liverpool and Ireland, with a programme which reflects the diversity of Irish culture. Highlights of the 24-day festival, which kicks off in October, have included concerts by Van Morrison, The Dubliners, Christy Moore and Hothouse Flowers, while other events include films, plays, traditional Irish music sessions and a Liverpool Irish Heritage coach tour.

LIVERPOOL MUSIC WEEK

www.liverpoolmusicweek.co.uk

Famous for its non-restricted musical policy, Liverpool Music Week features bands and artists from every genre including indie, rock, electronic, funk, soul, Latin, nu wave, jazz, and world music. The event, usually held in November each year, plays host to over 300 live bands in venues across the city. The festival format is a combination of ticketed shows and free shows, with artists including the UK's biggest live acts as well as new emerging talent. Previous signed acts include Super Furry Animals, Kasabian, The Specials, Goldfrapp, Vampire Weekend, Calvin Harris and Seasick Steve, while the festival's free music programme takes place across dozens of Liverpool's city-centre venues.

MATHEW STREET FESTIVAL

www.mathewstreetfestival.org

There cannot be many cities in Europe who can put on a successful event like Mathew Street Festival, year in, year out. During the weekend of August Bank Holiday, Liverpool becomes a party capital attracting hundreds of thousands into the city centre for the UK's biggest annual free outdoor music festival. With six outdoor stages and huge LED screens across the city, crowds flock to watch bands from across the musical spectrum. As well as the hugely popular Beatle impersonators and other tribute bands (Guns 2 Roses, Led Zed, Kaiser Thiefs, Amy Wynehouse, Razorlike ... you get the drift!) Mathew Street Festival features country and western, Irish and American-themed stages, and much more. The fringe festival continues to go from strength to strength, where Liverpool's hottest new bands play in the hippest venues.

Mathew Street Festival

SOUND CITY

www.liverpoolsoundcity.co.uk

With hundreds of gigs and a music industry conference to rival any on the planet, Liverpool Sound City is strong evidence that the city's music scene is in rude health. Drawing inspiration from the US festival South By South West, Liverpool Sound City showcases household names alongside tomorrow's young hopefuls. Held during May, bands play at locations large and small – from St George's Hall to bars and car parks. New for 2010, international music conference Musexpo Europe joins Sound City.

SOUTHPORT JAZZ FESTIVAL

www.visitsouthport.com

Get jazzed up for summer with this four-day event held in May each year. With a programme of up-and-coming musicians, seasoned performers and headline acts, the jazz festival always creates a buzz around Southport, encouraging people to get out and enjoy themselves, listening to music from performers from all over the world. Best of all, most of it is free. The Fringe section of the festival features a daily line-up of top performers across a number of smaller venues.

What's new Pussycat? The Summer Pops welcomes Tom Jones

SUMMER POPS

www.echoarena.com

Liverpool Summer Pops Festival is one of the biggest city music festivals in Europe and attracts some of the world's top stars in classical, pop and rock music to the ECHO Arena. The festival has played host to a diverse line-up of acts, from the Pussycat Dolls to Leonard Cohen, Pet Shop Boys and The Pogues. The event celebrates its tenth anniversary in 2010 and keeps getting bigger and better, with more shows, more venues and more styles to suit everyone. Special events and fringe festivals have included Beatles Day and the indie weekender.

THE WORLD ON A PLATE

Jane Haase, Emma Johnson and Jade Wright bring you the restaurants, bistros and cafés that our taste-testing team know and love.

CONTEMPORARY CUISINE

60 HOPE STREET
Liverpool L1 9BZ
0151 707 6060
www.60hopestreet.com

60 Hope Street has anchored the south end of Hope Street's cultural and foodie hub for well over a decade. Its modern British cooking is served, usually with a twist, and always with flair. Want a prime example? Look no further than their deep-fried jam buttie with Carnation milk ice cream. Delicious!

BLACKBURNE ARMS
4 Catharine Street
Liverpool L8 7NL
0151 707 1249

Don't misspell 'Blackburne' in your TomTom as you might end up travelling up the M65. Nestled in the Georgian quarter, Blackburne Arms has a patio area for summer drinks and wholesome pub food – including its renowned roast potatoes.

BLAKES AT HARD DAY'S NIGHT HOTEL
North John Street
Liverpool L2 6RX
0151 243 2121
www.harddaysnighthotel.com

All you need is grub – the menu at Liverpool's Beatle-themed restaurant is full of great flavours with a focus on seasonal, organic and locally sourced produce. For culture vultures, the interior décor and the name of the restaurant are inspired by pop artist Sir Peter Blake, who designed the Sgt Pepper album cover.

THE EXCHANGE
Hilton Hotel Liverpool
3 Thomas Steers Way
Liverpool ONE
0151 708 4200
www.hilton.co.uk/liverpool

The finest North West cuisine, sourced from a 40-mile radius. The restaurant seats 140, and we love the Goosnargh chicken breast, crispy leg with creamed cabbage, Formby mushroom and shallot sauce.

FRAICHE
11 Rose Mount
Oxton
Wirral CH43 5SG
0151 652 2914
www.restaurantfraiche.com

Chef Marc Wilkinson won Merseyside its first Michelin star in 2008. Fraiche won the coveted award for its modern French cuisine with a twist, and has also been awarded the best wine list of any UK restaurant by the Which Good Food Guide 2010. Book early, as tables are in demand.

JALONS BRIDEWELL
Campbell Square
Liverpool L1 5LB
0151 709 4195

There's quite something about sipping posh cocktails inside a prison cell. Jalons Bridewell, off Duke Street, is a converted Victorian prison which has been transformed into a chic bar and restaurant. The trademark cells have been left in all their splendour, while the restaurant upstairs has been tastefully redesigned to include a champagne lounge.

THE LIVING ROOM
15 Victoria St
Liverpool L2 5QS
0870 442 2535
www.thelivingroom.co.uk

Since it opened its doors in 2001 this trendy bar and restaurant has been a hit with Liverpool's in crowd. Dark and sexy, the restaurant is ideal for a romantic meal for two or a girls' night out. The menu boasts a host of classic favourites from chicken caesar salad to 100% beef burgers, to steak, ale and mushroom pie.

LONDON CARRIAGE WORKS
40 Hope Street
Liverpool L1 9DA
0151 705 2222
www.thelondoncarriageworks.co.uk

Situated in the Hope Street Hotel in Liverpool's Georgian Quarter, the London Carriage Works has established itself as one of the city's finest restaurants. Chef patron Paul Askew has won numerous awards and his insistence on the use of high quality, seasonal and locally sourced products wherever possible has become central to the identity of The London Carriage Works.

MALMAISON
William Jessop Way
Princes Dock
Liverpool L3 1QZ
0151 229 5000
www.malmaisonliverpool.com

Hotel restaurants tend to disappoint in atmosphere as well as the food but the Malmaison brasserie bucks the trend. It's a chic, welcoming dining room with natural light flooding in from the huge windows. The menu takes in upmarket, stylishly done favourites – pizzas, pastas, fish and chips – and the more adventurous – black pudding spring rolls, chicken liver parfait and toasted brioche with grape chutney. Insider recommends the Eton Mess, which is heavenly.

THE MONRO
92-94 Duke Street
Liverpool L1 5A
0871 811 4783
www.themonro.com

Named after a Georgian trading ship, The Monro is classed as one of Liverpool's first gastropubs, providing top-quality food in traditional pub surroundings. Treat yourself to The Monro's homemade shepherd's pie with cauliflower cheese or posh fish and chips with mushy peas, chunky chips and a homemade tartare sauce. Great comfort food with a cosy, homely feel and lots of roaring fires.

THE ORCHARD
57 Blundell Street
Liverpool L1 0AJ
0151 709 3060
www.theorchardliverpool.com

Cider is the cool people's choice nowadays, so you might want to pop to The Orchard and check out that menu – 18 different types of the stuff and every one of them a temptation. Other drinks are available, and The Orchard offers wholesome and hearty fare to complement them all.

OSQA
7-9 Oldham Street
Liverpool L1 2SU
0151 709 6611
www.osqa-restaurant.co.uk

OSQA offers fantastic live music played almost nightly, with good food and a friendly atmosphere. The wine is good, the food is delicious and the prices reasonable. And come summer, their outdoor terrace in the evening sunshine is heaven itself.

PANAM
Britannia Pavilion
Albert Dock L3 4AE
0151 702 5840
www.panam-venue.co.uk

One of the first bars to set up home in the converted warehouses of the Albert Dock nigh on a decade ago, PanAm has stood the test of time and remains one of the city's favourite hangouts. On the food front they offer a full internationally-flavoured a la carte menu, bistro fare and even a kids' menu and pre-concert menu for those off to catch an arena show.

PUSCHKA
16 Rodney Street
Liverpool L1 2TE
0151 707 9772
www.puschka.co.uk

Sandwiched between rows of some of the area's finest houses in Rodney Street, Puschka prides itself on offering the best of modern British cuisine, albeit served alongside some colourful Mediterranean offerings. But book early – Puschka is devilishly popular – and rightly so.

THE RESTAURANT BAR & GRILL
Halifax House
Brunswick Street
Liverpool L2 0UU
0151 236 6703
www.therestaurantbarandgrill.co.uk

A spacious venue with a striking cocktail bar in its centre and dining booths and tables either side, it is popular with the post-work crowd.

ST JOHN RESTAURANT
24 Sir Thomas Street
Liverpool L1 6JB
0151 236 1366
www.sirthomashotel.co.uk

It is not hard to see why film stars and football legends would choose this restaurant to hang out in. It is undeniably luxurious, all red leather seats, banquettes and some of the most private booth seating in Liverpool.

SIMPLY HEATHCOTES
Beetham Plaza
25 The Strand
Liverpool L2 0XL
0151 236 3536
www.heathcotes.co.uk

Paul Heathcote was the first celebrity chef to blaze a trail improving the culinary offerings of Liverpool. The Simply Heathcotes menu features Goosnargh chicken, hand selected cuts of matured English lamb and beef from pedigree stock and artisan cheeses as well as seasonal fruit and vegetables.

ZIBA
The Racquet Club
5 Chapel Street
Liverpool L3 9AG
0151 236 6676

A tasteful combination of the classical and contemporary. The head chef and his brigade focus on quality, fresh local produce and source many ingredients from the organic Home Farm shop at the Eagle & Child in Bispham Green – the menu is described as 'modern English with a twist'. The food is consistently good and the service faultlessly courteous and attentive without being intrusive.

The big breakfast

AS your mum more than likely told you, there's nothing like a hearty breakfast to start the day and we couldn't agree more. So here are some of Liverpool's top brekkies...

THE TAVERN COMPANY
621 Smithdown Road
Penny Lane L15 5AG
0151 734 5555

Perhaps best known for its tasty Mexican fayre, The Tavern Co, near Penny Lane, easily romps its way into our best breakfast venues. A popular weekend hangout for families, friends and couples alike, the restaurant's bustling atmosphere, free tea and coffee refills and mouth-watering menu are an instant hit. House dishes include doorstop French toast, toasted bagel with cream cheese and the mighty American complete with fluffy pancake. The restaurant is open for brunch from 10.30am to 2.30pm on Saturday and 10am to 2.30pm on Sunday.

KIMOS
38-44 Mount Pleasant
Liverpool L3 5SX
0151 707 8288

A welcoming Mediterranean restaurant, Kimos brings a new twist to breakfast time and serves a plethora of dishes from 10am to 5pm seven days a week. Whether you fancy the Foule Mudammas (traditional Arabic breakfast), fluffy omelettes or Mediterranean breakfast with fresh tomatoes, feta cheese, olives, falafels, fried egg and warm pitta bread, it's enough to satisfy even the biggest breakfast craving.

STUDIO 2
33-45 Parr Street
Liverpool L1 4JN
0151 707 1050
www.parrstreet.co.uk
Ian Cook, TV's Come Dine With Me Liverpool champion, is in charge of catering here – and it shows. There are the old favourites, like the full English, but there are also more unusual options like the Studio Americana and the Salmon Benedict. They also do a veggie breakfast and a vegan breakfast.

THE MOON AND PEA
64 Lark Lane
Liverpool L17 8UU
0151 727 6282
www.themoonandpea.co.uk
Breakfast treats include Belgian waffles, Eggs Florentine and both veggie and vegan full breakfasts. For a real belly buster try the Moon breakfast, with double egg, sausage, bacon and toast, plus mushrooms, tomato, black pudding, beans and homefries.

THE PILGRIM
Pilgrim Street
Liverpool L1 9HB
0151 709 2302
A firm favourite with students and locals alike, washing away their hangovers with a morning tipple or triple. A cheap and cheerful underground haunt.

Bless this Scouse

SCOUSE is a dish – a people and an accent.

Before the term 'Scouse' came along Liverpool sailors were called Dickie Sams named after a famous tavern in the town. Then Norwegian sailors created a dish called lab or lob-skause. Well, Norwegians would!

Mersey sailors adopted it and the skause - in nasal translation became Scouse. Seafarers and their families made this nutritious dish part of their diets. Liverpool folk still swear by it. The Scouse meal consists of meat, vegetables and potatoes served with red cabbage or beetroot and crusty bread.

It can be dished out piping hot or be ready made and kept for up to two days covered in a refrigerator and re-heated in a saucepan. Most people prefer the added depth of flavour that re-heating adds. If a spoon can stand-up in the centre of the pot it is, as we say on Merseyside, truly fab. Blind Scouse is ideal for veggies – it doesn't have the meat.

As someone who has sampled Scouse throughout childhood and adulthood, I still say no one makes Scouse "like me ma".

But the following eateries come pretty close to the dish we've known for all these years.

Here are PG's Tips. But anywhere you see the sign 'Scouse' try it.

- Maggie May's, Bold Street
- Jamie Carragher's Sports Café in Stanley Street and his Express place in Liverpool ONE
- Ma Boyle's Oyster House in Tower Gardens near St Nick's church
- Hope Street Hotel in Hope Street
- The trendy Newz Bar run by the Flanagan brothers who sure know their Scouse

Peter Grant

ITALIAN

CASA BELLA

25 Victoria Street
Liverpool L1 6BD
0151 258 1800
www.casabellarestaurant.co.uk

Italian born ex-chef Franco Furlani manages this popular Italian restaurant, bringing a real continental feel combined with a friendly and relaxed atmosphere. The restaurant serves more than 15 types of pizza along with a broad range of pasta dishes and classic Italian fish and meat dishes. There are also daily specials and an extensive a la carte menu.

ITALIAN CLUB FISH

128 Bold Street
Liverpool L1 4JA
0151 707 2110

Italian Club Fish does cracking cocktails, and, unsurprisingly, superb fish. Proprietor Rosaria Crolla combines her Italian heritage with her Scottish roots, and a menu that twins high quality UK fish and chips with Italian-style shellfish, oysters and pasta dishes. Ask for a Robert De Nero or an Al Pacino cocktail and sit back and sip in true Godfather style.

IL FORNO

132 Duke Street
Liverpool L1 5AG
0151 709 4002
www.ilforno.co.uk

A large, bustling Italian with a huge real flame pizza oven, Il Forno has become a hit with celebrities and Premiership footballers alike. Not to mention visiting Italians who want a real taste of home.

PICCOLINO

14a Cook St
Liverpool L2 9RF
0151 236 2555
www.piccolinorestaurants.co.uk

Located in the heart of the Liverpool business quarter, this is the sort of restaurant where contacts are made and deals are done. But you don't have to be having a working lunch to take advantage of this established restaurant, serving a wonderful combination of both modern and classic Italian dishes. Look out for the daily specials menu and a menu del giorno served from noon every day.

THE QUARTER

7 Falkner Street
Liverpool L8 7PU
0151 707 1965
www.thequarteruk.com.

A meeting place all day long, The Quarter's unique atmosphere and great value for money attracts a variety of guests from businessmen to bohemians. The main menu features a number of pasta and pizza dishes, that range from traditional Italian favourites to Thai, Greek and Spanish options. There are daily specials and the sweet cabinet boasts a varied and impressive array of cakes and desserts to tempt any palate. Open from 8am Monday to Friday and 10am on weekends, The Quarter is also the perfect place for a delicious breakfast.

SAN CARLO

41 Castle Street
Liverpool L2 9SH
0151 236 0073
www.sancarlo.co.uk/liverpool

San Carlo is the kind of establishment that demands a fresh haircut, polished shoes and clean fingernails. It's not the biggest restaurant in the city but what it lacks in size it makes up for in style and a moreish menu laden with quality fish dishes and, naturally, plenty of pasta. The wine list is very Italian inspired while the array of beers available is also typical of any establishment you'd find on the streets of Rome or Milan.

VILLA ROMANA
6 Wood Street
Liverpool L1 4AQ
0151 708 8004
www.villa-romana.co.uk

This warm, cosy, rustic Italian has built up a loyal following over the years and diners keep coming back for its unpretentious and reasonably priced, authentic Italian food. It's a popular bustling restaurant where you can expect good service and a menu full of tasty Italian dishes, including a very tempting sweet trolley.

ZELIG'S
Thomas Steers Way
Liverpool ONE L1 8LW
0151 709 7097
www.zeligs.co.uk

Leonard Zelig, the fictional proprietor, may have first made his name mixing it with various social classes of 1920s New York courtesy of Woody Allen, but his big break into the gastro world starts here. Quirky and flamboyant, Zelig's is a huge, cavernous building with a downstairs bar and a restaurant above. The menu features Italian dishes from Spaghetti Marinara & Beef Carpaccio to stone-baked pizzas. As intimate as it is grand and the number one spot for post-shopping summer drinks.

Family friendly

TAKING the kids out for a bite to eat can be a challenge, as some restaurateurs will see devil's horns on your little angel when you bring them in.

But although they might not appreciate the extra crumbs dropped on the floor, not to mention the running around and loud singing of the Timmy Time theme tune, there are plenty of eateries which will welcome you and your family with open arms. One of the most child-friendly venues has to be Wagamama in Liverpool ONE. This Pan Asian noodle restaurant has a really relaxed seating arrangement with communal tables and benches with room for the whole family and chairs for small children which clip onto the table so they can be right next to mum and dad and feel part of the action.

There's a healthy choice of fresh, nutritious, MSG-free dishes, cooked to order and your little Picassos can noodle doodle to their hearts' content with colouring books and crayons provided to keep them entertained.

The Olive Press on Castle Street (pictured) has a fab choice of healthy foods on its kids' menu and is a great place for the credit-crunch afflicted as children can enjoy a main course, dessert and a drink for just £4.95. Youngsters even have their own Little Olives reward card which entitles them to a special gift once they have completed a series of culinary tasks.

Also encouraging the budding Gordon Ramsays of tomorrow, Gusto at the Albert Dock gives kids the chance to make their own pizzas. For £5.95 each mini pizza chef is given a chef's hat and pizza base with a choice of toppings to create your own perfect pizza.

Meanwhile, over at the PanAm at the Albert Dock, kids eat free during school holidays when eating with a paying adult and they can be all grown up and sip children's cocktails or 'mocktails' as they are called (alcohol free of course!)

Michelle Rushton

FRENCH

BISTRO FRANC
Church House
1 Hanover Street
Liverpool L1 3DW
0151 708 9993
www.bistrofranc.com

The latest from owners of the popular Bistro Pierre, on Button Street in the Cavern Quarter, and Bistro Jacques on Hardman Street. The menu is with a hint towards modern English rather than pure classic French. A selection of delicious duck, chicken, fish, lamb and fillet steak dishes sit alongside the vegetarian options, all reasonably priced. Bistro Franc is already getting a similar following to its bigger brothers and has the same weekly and early bird specials, which offer three courses and wine at penny-pinching prices.

GREEN ROOM
95 Banks Road
West Kirby CH48 0RB
0871 811 4723

The Green Room in West Kirby is another French bistro adhering to the simple rustic Gallic look. With its wooden floors, exposed brickwork and art it is cosy and romantic. The bistro-style menu changes every three months to keep in with the seasons. There is plenty of choice, without the menu being over-facing, and the staff are attentive.

SPANISH

LA VIÑA
11-15 North John Street
Liverpool L2 5QY
0151 255 1401
www.lavina.co.uk

Naturally you will find plenty of tapas dishes here, but La Viña offers much more of a taste of Spain than just patatas bravas. The menu is split into montados (tapas on small bread), paellas, brochetas (meat or vegetables on skewers), meat and fish tapas, vegetable tapas, main courses, cured meats and salads. There is also a wide selection of breads and some fantastic desserts. Great atmosphere and top-class service.

TAPAS TAPAS
14 Back Colquitt Street
Arthouse Square
Liverpool L1 4DE
0151 709 0999
www.tapastapas.co.uk

This restaurants brings a bit of Mediterranean sunshine to Merseyside – the kind of place you really don't want to leave once you're ensconced with a nice bottle of Rioja. The main menu is divided into Spanish delicacies – mainly hams and cheeses – village, coastal and countryside tapas, house specialities and various paellas. Look out for the special offers too.

LUNYA
18-20 College Lane
Liverpool L1 3DS
0151 706 9770
www.lunya.co.uk

Touted as the country's first 'Catalonian fusion deli and restaurant', Lunya offers a selection of a la carte and tapas food to choose from, or even small snacks to dabble with while enjoying a drink. Although the Catalonian-connection seems a little hazy – Lunya is the brainchild of a Wirral businessman who loves Spain – the menu features pages and pages of delicious tapas, and a huge selection of fine Spanish wines.

MEDITERRANEAN

ALAMIR BISTRO
93 Eastbank Street
Southport PR8 1DG
01704 544615
www.alamirbistro.com

Nestled among the carpet shops and tyre fitters on Southport's Eastbank Street you will find this unassuming Lebanese restaurant and be glad you did. This cosy eaterie (it only holds 26 diners) is all mirrors, warm, peachy terracotta walls and bright postcards featuring the Lebanon's historic splendours. Specialities include mazza, the Lebanese version of Greek mezze. Newcomers to Lebanese food could opt for one of the plentiful set menu options.

ACCHUS TAVERNA
4 Waterloo Road
iverpool L3 7BB
151 255 1661
ww.bacchustaverna.co.uk

acchus may be off the eaten track tucked between iverpool's converted arehouses but sitting under nes, looking at the eascapes and listening to ne sound of bazoukis in the ackground, you will feel like ou have been transported way to Athens. The menu is love song to Greek national shes and they are done ery well. Try the Gairdes stin cara, kleftiko psito, or if you ant to be more traditional, e moussaka. If you can find om, don't leave without ying the Baclava cake.

CHRISTAKIS GREEK TAVERNA
7 York Street
Liverpool L1 5BN
0151 708 7377
www.christakisgreektaverna.com

Expect great food and fun at Christakis, specialising in traditional Greek food and with entertainment too. At weekends they offer Greek dancing, plate smashing and belly dancing with a DJ until 2am and various party banquet options. Not a night for wallflowers!

ELIF
6 Lark Lane
Liverpool L17 8US
0151 728 7362

Aigburth's Turkish barbecue restaurant is a small, no-nonsense sort of place that is usually packed with diners enjoying their meals behind enormous floor-to-ceiling glass windows as you walk past. Elif offers a back-to-basics approach to food – the menu consisting mostly of large portions of flame-grilled meat – that is simply mouth-watering. Busy and noisy.

SAKARA BAR & RESTAURANT
372 Aigburth Road
Liverpool L17 6AE
0151 427 2200

This Egyptian-themed bar and restaurant, just two minutes from Aigburth station, is a real suburban hotspot. The welcome from the staff at the family-run eaterie is as warm as the fabulous Asian, African and Middle Eastern-inspired dishes they serve up. On the food front portions are plentiful and the mezze dishes come highly recommended to get a true flavour of the cuisine.

ZORBAS
1 Leece Street
Liverpool L1 2TR
0151 709 0190
www.zorbasrestaurant.co.uk

Owner Michael Haralambos opened Zorbas more than 30 years ago and this family-run restaurant prides itself on giving diners a big fat Greek welcome. The food is as traditional as it comes and you will find the likes of stuffed vine leaves among the dozen or so vegetarian starters and Tsoutsoukakia for the meat lovers out there.

CHINESE

CITY RENDEZVOUS
2 Columbus Quay
Riverside Drive
Liverpool L3 4DB
0151 726 8191

Still known to many as the Chung Ku, the City Rendezvous Restaurant is instantly recognisable for its utterly modern architectural design, impressive structure and its eye-popping views out over the Mersey and Wirral. Food here is rather universally regarded as 'top notch'. The fact that you see many Chinese customers here, be that for weddings, functions or simply family meals, is testimony enough.

MA BO
16 Nelson St
Liverpool L1 5DN
0151 709 4551

If you want a no-frills, authentic Chinese experience then make it Ma Bo. There are no huge flashing signs or fussy lighting, no fancy tablecloths and no fancy wine list – in fact, no wine, unless you take it with you (no corkage charge either.) A slice of true Shanghai. Try the wonton char sui noodle soup – delicious.

THE MANDARIN
73-79 Victoria Street
Liverpool L1 6DE
0151 227 9011
www.mandarinliverpool.co.uk

A family run restaurant, the Mandarin is a stunning venue with its stained glass and

tropical fish and has a longstanding reputation for quality food and service. The menu seems endless and the portions huge – the Cantonese style fried sliced steak, served on a sizzling hot platter, is a dish to remember, while the baked lobster tails with ginger and spring onion or black bean sauce are well worth forking out a little bit more for.

MEI MEI
9-13 Berry Street
Liverpool L1 9DF
0151 707 2888

This large Chinese restaurant right on the edge of Liverpool's Chinatown is one of the city's most stylish. The menu is extensive and largely Cantonese. There are plenty of familiar dishes as well as the more exotic like scallop with tofu in a black bean sauce or cai sun, a spinach/asparagus-style Chinese vegetable cooked with garlic, and dumplings consisting of baby bamboo mixed with prawn.

NORTH GARDEN
28 Nelson Street
Liverpool L1 5DN
0151 709 4247

Tucked away on Nelson Street, North Garden is a fabulous little restaurant, with great, authentic tasting Chinese dishes and excellent service. Try the braised halibut hot pot and order a pot of Chinese tea to wash it down with. Don't be surprised if your bill comes in at as little as £25. Great for a nibble after a night on the tiles as it stays open until the small hours.

YUET BEN
1 Upper Duke Street
Liverpool L1 9DU
0151 709 5772
www.yuetben.co.uk

One of Liverpool's oldest and most revered Chinese restaurants, Yuet Ben was opened in 1968 by Shandong-born Yuh Ho Yau and originally stood on Great George Street. These days it is run by Yuh's daughter Theresa and her husband who make it their mission to bring to Liverpool authentic tastes and flavours of Northern Chinese cuisine. The venue itself is far from fancy but you don't need shiny lights and designer furniture when your food is this good, plus choose the right table and you will get a fabulous view of the Chinese Arch. Insider recommends the barbecue spare ribs and the crepes with mandarins and Cointreau.

Veggie heaven

LIVERPOOL has some wonderful vegetarian eateries, worlds away from the dishes that pass for the veggie option in most restaurants – essentially just meat-and-two-veg, minus the meat.

Lying in Newington, off Bold Street, The Egg Café (pictured) is well worth a short detour. The air inside is deliciously filled with the mouth-watering aromas of gorgeous food and the dazzling array of hot and cold dishes on display at the counter. All are vegetarian, and most vegan too. Bliss. Egg is a Godsend for vegetarians who want choice – and ones with an appetite that a salad won't satisfy. There's a range of hearty, wintry, dishes on offer – including homemade burger, rather than a fresh-from-the-freezer beanburger, and huge doorstops of quiche.

For a veggie roast try The Richmond Tavern in Wavertree or Keith's Wine Bar on Lark Lane, which are always packed on a Sunday – just down the road on Lark Lane you'll also find Green Days, which has some great veggie options on offer too. The Baltic Fleet pub on Wapping, offers a good three-course Sunday vegetarian roast and, of course, lovely beers.

Sam and Joe's Internet Café on South Hunter Street, just off Hardman Street, does an excellent breakfast, as does Leaf on Parliament Street or Amber on Rose Lane, Mossley Hill.

Vegetarians are well-catered for at Delifonseca on Stanley Street and the lentil and potato moussaka is one of the restaurant's signature dishes.

Thailand remains one of the most devoutly Buddhist countries in the world, so many dishes at Chaophraya are vegetarian – in 2008 the restaurant was chosen by The Times newspaper as the best vegetarian restaurant in the UK. Yuet Ben, near the Chinese Arch, also offers a separate vegetarian menu.

At Berry Street's noodle bar Tokyou, all the noodles are made fresh each day and with a mix of Korean, Japanese and Cantonese food, there are a few vegetarian options on offer.

Maharaja, on London Road, serves food from the south of India, specifically Kerala state. This coastal region is known for its vegetarian dishes and spices and all feature prominently on a menu that is a million miles away from your typical curry house fare.

Finally, if you are looking for some tasty veggie food on the go, check out Souper Food on Rumford Street, in the business district. The daily-changing menu features mouth-watering homemade specials suitable for a variety of dietary requirements – all high quality, fairtrade and organic 'fast' food.

PAN ASIAN & JAPANESE

ETSU
25 The Strand
Liverpool L2 0XJ
0151 236 7530
www.etsu-restaurant.co.uk

Tucked away in a somewhat quiet corner of Liverpool city centre but definitely worth seeking out for its authentic Japanese food in a cosy and relaxed environment. If you are looking for an intro to Japanese food this is a good place to start as it offers the full range from sushi and sashimi to steak and chicken dishes via tempura and noodles, and they do bento boxes at lunchtimes. If you are feeling adventurous you could even try the unagi don – grilled eel to you and me!

HOST
31 Hope Street
Liverpool L1 9HX
0151 708 5831
www.ho-st.co.uk

This East-meets-West Pan-Asian fusion restaurant may have something of a utilitarian feel to it with the hard benches and minimal décor but that only ensures all the focus is on the food. And it is worth focusing on. The menu is made up of rice, noodle, soup and fish dishes from the likes of China, Thailand, Malaysia and Japan. Insider recommends the crab and sweet potato cakes with wasabi mayo, and the green chicken curry with Thai aubergine.

MATOU
George's Parade, Pier Head
Liverpool L3 1BY
0151 236 2928
www.matou.co.uk

Opened on the top floor of the Pier Head's Mersey Ferry terminal building, Matou is a modern pan Asian restaurant, cocktail bar and lounge. The menu merges dishes from the Far East including Malaysia, Thailand, Singapore, Japan, China and includes a tempting selection of signature fusion dishes.

SAPPORO TEPPANYAKI
134 Duke Street
Liverpool L1 5AG
0151 705 3005
www.sapporo.co.uk

At Sapporo you don't just get a meal, you get gastronomic theatre. Although there are also plenty of sushi and noodle dishes on offer, the teppanyaki grill is what it's all about here as chefs chop, fry and juggle your food on the flaming hot-plate right before your eyes. The set combinations start with the Ninja, featuring Namasu salad, miso wakame soup, tuna maki rolls, chicken teriyaki, grilled vegetables, fried rice, potatoes and fruit salad. If you really feel like going wild try the Emperor combination for a minimum of six people.

THE SUSHI BAR
The Vincent Hotel
98 Lord Street
Southport PR8 1JR
01704 883800

At the stylish Vincent Hotel you can dine on the finest handmade sushi, tasty miso soup and freshly cut sashim in uber-glamorous surroundings. Order the sush and sashimi individually fron the a la carte menu or sampl a platter with a chilled bottle of Kirin Japanese beer.

WAGAMAMA
Liverpool ONE
Liverpool L1 8JF
0151 707 2762
www.wagamama.com

If you are looking for fabulou noodles in a relaxed setting Wagamama is the place. The restaurant's philosophy is fresh and nutritious food in an elegant yet simple setting with helpful, friendly service and value for money and tha pretty much describes what you get. Wagamama is modelled on the popular Japanese ramen bars and dining is communal style meaning you sit on long benches with other customers. Be warned, they serve food when it is ready so don't be shocked if dishes come out at different times. Just go with it!

THAI

HAOPHRAYA
enyon Steps
iverpool ONE L1 3DF
151 707 6323
ww.chaophraya.co.uk

naophraya (pronounced now-Pie-A) has a ommanding location on the p deck of Liverpool ONE. ut it's the food that's the real ar here. Try the gaeng pa, hich is about as hot as it ets – a fantastic Thai jungle urry, flavoured with digenous herbs, bamboo noots, green beans, holy asil, green pepper, baby corn nd lesser galangal. It's made ith a choice of pork, nicken, beef or prawns, and ey say its hotness burns f calories on its own.

HILLI BANANA
Lark Lane
verpool L17 8US
151 726 8641
ww.chillibanana.co.uk

xpect a warm welcome at nilli Banana because the am at this popular restaurant was awarded 'Taste Liverpool 08' accreditation for excellence in food and customer service. Desserts include banana split, banana ice cream, and yes, chilli banana.

SABAI
26 North John Street
Liverpool L2 9RU
0151 236 7655

The only downside of Sabai is that with an almost endless collection of all manner of green and red curries, Sabai specials, Thai salads and stir fries it could take you a while to decide what to have. Not that the unfailingly polite and courteous staff will mind in the least, Sabai actually means "to relax or chill out" and the ever-smiling waiters and waitresses here do their very best to ensure you do exactly that.

INDIAN

THE GULSHAN
544-548 Aigburth Road
Liverpool L19 3QG
0151 427 2273
www.gulshan-liverpool.com

Founded by Mustafa and Salina Rahman in 1986, this award-winning restaurant has built up quite a reputation. The Gulshan has a downstairs restaurant and a tapas and cocktail bar upstairs. Expect to see many curry favourites on the menu but also a host of excellent chef specials and a good range of vegetarian options. Insider recommends the lamb green balti massalla, one of The Gulshan's signature dishes.

THE LIGHT OF BENGAL
286-288 Aigburth Road
Liverpool L17 9PW
0151 728 7030

The Light of Bengal knows the way to a curry lover's heart is to get the basics right – but the staff here can't resist throwing in a few more unusual offerings too. You could throw caution to the wind and try the salmon curry but there are plenty of other tempting dishes too, including the chicken tikka exotica and the Nawabi chicken in Chef's Special massala.

INDIAN

MAHARAJA
34-36 London Road
Liverpool L3 5NF
0871 811 4798
www.maharajaliverpool.co.uk

An Indian with a difference, Maharaja serves food from the south of the subcontinent, specifically Kerala state. This coastal region is known for its seafood, vegetarian dishes and spices and all feature prominently on a menu that is a million miles away from your typical curry house fare. You could try the prawn mango curry or maybe the squid olathu which will see you served sliced squid cooked in a green massala and coconut sauce with those all important spices. The mixed lentil curry is also a good option.

MAYUR
130 Duke Street
Liverpool L1 5AG
0151 709 9955
www.mayurrestaurant.co.uk

At Mayur, the service is first class from the moment you walk through the glass doors. Courteous and attentive staff usher you to your table and you never have to flag anyone down to get a top-up on your drink, your plates cleared or the bill. Opened by a family of doctors, the ethos is one of high-quality food served in a healthy way. A large part of the menu focuses on cuisine using the Tandoor oven, where bread, fish, meat and game are all cooked in the authentic North West Indian style which is low in oils and fat. There are also curries and creative chef specials.

SPICE LOUNGE
Albert Dock
Liverpool L3 4AE
0151 707 2202
www.spicelounge.uk.com

A stone's throw from the ECHO arena this stylish venue offers a delicious array of modern Indian cuisine. Opened by restaurateur Ali Noor after making a success of two popular restaurants in Woolton Village and Hunts Cross, his aim is to provide "proper Indian dishes" – the food that people are really eating on the hot streets of Delhi and Rajasthan and the beaches of Goa. For authenticity, he imports spices every two months direct from India, which he grinds and roasts every day. Expect to pay more than you usual curry but it's worth it.

SULTAN'S PALACE
75-77 Victoria Street
Liverpool L1 6DE
0151 227 9020
www.sultans-palace.co.uk

Most Merseyside curry fans will know the hugely popular Sultan's Palace, a family-run restaurant in Victoria Street. The chefs here make an effo to improve all those familiar favourites while throwing a few wild cards onto the menu too. Specials include the Narial Gosht, lamb sautéed with coconut and mixed garl and ginger and their secret blend of spices and the Rara Gosht Punjabi – the restaurant's own creation of minced and diced lamb with that all important kick.

UNI
67 Renshaw Street
Liverpool L1 2SJ
0151 7096587

While much debate surrounc the pronunciation of its nam (It's pronounced 'You – n – Eye" for those in the "Yuni" camp) UnI is a firm favourite with those frequenting the city's curry quarter. The service is quick and friendly even if you hide yourself in a booth with the curtains drawn (don't forget your dimmer switch and service bell). Popular dishes include the giant meat samosas anc seek kebab with the Cha Cha King Prawn Special and Naz's Special – chicken and potatoes and pilau rice.

A ROOM WITH A VIEW

CHAOPHRAYA
Kenyon Steps
Liverpool ONE
0151 707 6323
www.chaophraya.co.uk

Arguably the most popular restaurant to emerge from Liverpool One, Chaophraya has a commanding location perched on the top deck with views of the Albert Dock. Chaophraya really has the wow factor – floor to ceiling windows offer incredible views across the city's docks and waterfront while also sucking in tons of natural light and thrilling sunsets.

FILINI
Radisson Blu Hotel
107 Old Hall Street
Liverpool L3 9BD
0151 966 1500
www.radissonblu.co.uk

The award-winning Filini restaurant has some of the most enviable waterfront views anywhere. The menu offers modern Italian food, taking the best local and Italian produce, merging them together to create mouth-watering, exquisite dishes to tantalise your taste buds.

MARITIME DINING ROOMS
Albert Dock
Liverpool L3 4AQ
0151 478 4056
www.liverpoolmuseums.org.uk

Situated on the fourth floor of the Merseyside Maritime Museum, this Michelin recommended restaurant with a menu devised by executive chef Nigel Paul Smith, offers window views on each flank. Its location means it effectively slices Liverpool in two – the new on one half, overlooking Liverpool ONE, and the old dock warehouses on the other. It would be hard to imagine a more beautiful contrasting view of the city, especially on a sunny day.

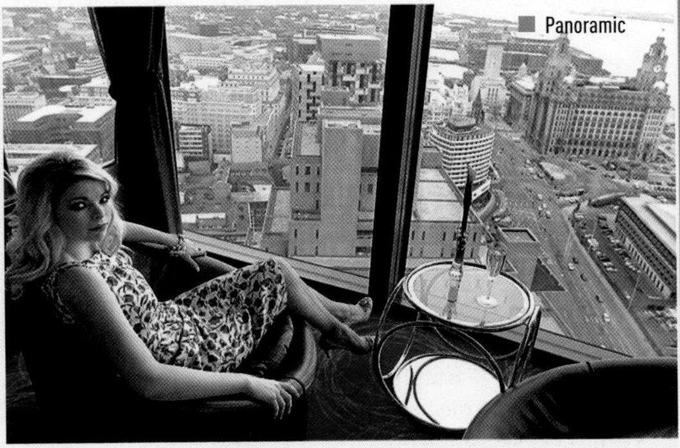
Panoramic

PANORAMIC
34th Floor West Tower
Brook Street
Liverpool L3 9PJ
0151 236 5534
www.panoramicliverpool.com

Britain's highest restaurant is the best way to see the city, and over to North Wales, Southport and Manchester. As the restaurant is approximately 300ft above sea level there is no gas allowed in the building so Chef Chris Marshall has to cook everything in water-baths. He takes it all in his stride. The food is legendary – celebrity diners include Kanye West, Steven Gerrard, Sir Paul McCartney and Katy Perry, but the biggest star is the view.

SHELDRAKES
Banks Road
Lower Heswall
Wirral CH60 9JS
0151 342 155
www.sheldrakesrestaurant.co.uk

Sheldrake's website boasts "view to dine for" and we are not arguing with the claim for one minute. As dinner vistas go the one on offer here – right across the River Dee to the Welsh Hills – takes some beating. A former sailing club, Sheldrakes is a charming place, and in the summer you can experience the Sheldrakes barbecue on the restaurant's delightful terrace.

THE AMERICAS

ALMA DE CUBA
St Peter's Church
Seel Street
Liverpool L1 4BH
0151 702 7394
www.alma-de-cuba.com

Housed in the former Catholic Church of St Peter's, Alma de Cuba is a fantastic venue. The church has been converted magnificently and retains the grand altar and religious iconography. The cuisine in the upstairs restaurant is an eclectic mix of Hispanic, Caribbean and South American flavours, with a tapas, lunch and a la carte menu. The gospel brunch, where you can enjoy singing from the choir alongside your meal from noon until 6pm every Sunday, is also highly recommended.

THE JAMES MONRO
69 Tithebarn Street
Liverpool L2 2EN
0151 236 9700
www.thejamesmonro.com

Promises authentic New York indulgence "from Little Italy to the Latin Quarter to the American Great Plains" and, while there is no steam coming up from the pavements outside, they sure have the Big Apple's flavours nailed.

LA CUBANITA
2 Campbell Street
Liverpool L1 5AX
0151 709 5335

Tucked away in Liverpool's Campbell Square, La Cubanita is a restaurant and bar where you can enjoy great Latin food and listen to some of the best live bands. Cuban cuisine is a fusion of Spanish, African and Caribbean cooking, something which is quickly evident when you see the menus – try the Vaca Frita, crispy strips of beef in a Cuban mojo marinade of roast garlic and lime juice, or the skewers of chicken and chorizo from the grill.

LAS IGUANAS
Liverpool ONE L1 8JF
0151 709 4030
www.iguanas.co.uk

An eclectic, lively mix of native Latin American, Indian, Spanish, Portuguese and African dishes. The signature dish, called Xinxim, is Brazilian lime chicken in a creamy crayfish and peanut sauce with rice, fine beans and sweet plantain and, intriguingly, it's also Pele's favourite grub.

SAVINA
138 Duke Street
Liverpool L1 5AG
0151 708 9095
www.savinarestaurant.co.uk

If you love Mexican then Savina is a must-visit. All the favourite dishes from south of the border are present from fabulous fajitas burstin with chicken or beef to enchiladas and burritos. Starters range from nachos and dips to pescados de chipotle – scallops marinate in white wine. Insider recommends the T-bone marinated in chilli and the Quebradizo on the dessert menu – chocolate wrapped i a cinnamon and honey dusted tortilla.

VALPARAISO
4 Hardman Street
Liverpool L1 9AX
0151 708 6036

This restaurant was opened in 1985 by Chilean consul Julio Arellano and is a romantic little place in the heart of Hardman Street. The menu changes often but is packed with traditional Chilean dishes including spicy and hearty stews, paella and pastel del choclo – a typical Chilean dish of minced beef topped with minced sweet corn.

LIGHT BITES

AFÉ SPORTS ENGLAND
2-44 Stanley Street
iverpool L1 6AL
ww.cafesportsengland.com
amie Carragher's family estaurant with a healthy vist is in a league of its own. omes off as a mix between a aditional sports bar, with big asma screens all over the alls, and a TGI Fridays with g bars, polished wood floors d banquette seating. As ou might expect of a place wned by an LFC favourite, ere is plenty of football emorabilia dotted about. It's e type of place where veryone's welcome, specially kids, who love the ealthy eating pizzas and moothies.

ELIFONSECA
2 Stanley Street
verpool L1 6AF
151 255 0808
ww.delifonseca.co.uk
elifonseca combines the est deli offerings with an xcellent restaurant and has arnered a clutch of awards. e menu includes verything from light bites to andwiches and salads, as ell as daily specials.

DDIE ROCKET'S
3 Bold Street
verpool L1 4DN
151 707 2500
ith its fabulous music, 50s tro feel, and fast and endly service, Eddie ocket's makes a great fun ternative to a formal restaurant meal. The menu includes thick and creamy shakes and malts, mouth-watering burgers, salads, sandwiches, nachos and hot dogs. They're open late too – until 4am Friday and Saturday – offering an altogether brighter alternative to queuing in a takeaway full of worse-for-wear lager louts past the witching hour.

EVERYMAN BISTRO
5-9 Hope Street
Liverpool L1 9BH
0151 708 9545
www.everyman.co.uk
Located beneath the famous theatre where actors like Julie Walters and Pete Postlethwaite learned their craft, the Everyman Bistro is something of a Liverpool institution. It's been around for more than 35 years and serves good quality home-cooked fare. Combined with a great atmosphere it's an unbeatable combination. Food is delicious and very reasonably priced and you can get three fantastic courses for about £15.

THE ITALIAN CLUB
85 Bold Street
Liverpool L1 4HF
0151 708 5508
www.theitalianclubliverpool.co.uk
A self-styled deli-restaurant, The Italian Club prides itself on offering dishes prepared and eaten as the Italians themselves would. The counter of beautiful salads and marinated vegetables and hot freshly prepared specials – not to mention the array of cakes – is mesmerizing. Perfect for a leisurely lunch.

SAHARAA
Arrad Street
Liverpool L7 7HX
0151 706 0111
This authentic – and wildly decorated – Lebanese restaurant, on a small road behind The Everyman, could be one of Liverpool's best-kept secrets. The food is delicious, fresh and good-sized portions, with some interesting variations on the usual hummous, fattoush, tabouleh, shish and kafta dishes. Mix and match some mezzes and pop open a bottle of plonk – it's a BYO. Cheap, cheerful and tasty.

THE SIDE DOOR
29 Hope Street
Liverpool L1 9BQ
0151 707 7888
www.thesidedoor.co.uk
The Side Door has been feeding hungry concert-goers for years. Pop in before a play at the Everyman or a concert at the Phil and enjoy their excellent, home-cooked food.

Café culture

NOWHERE does café culture better than Liverpool and that's a fact.

There is a long-running tradition of café culture in the city from the bustling milk bars of the 50s and the trendy hangouts of the 60s such as the Armadillo on Mathew Street, right through to today's stylish café.

Something of an institution, Café Tabac on Bold Street is one of the city's longest established cafes and has gone through a number of transformations during its long and varied history. Frequented by students and trendy bohemian types, it's the ideal place to 'sit off', enjoy a cup of coffee and discuss the issues of the day. The Bluecoat Chambers was always a popular venue for ardent café goers in the city and though the café has undergone a complete reincarnation and is now Espresso at the Bluecoat, the friendly ambience remains the same. If you want to sip with the hip, then tea is very much becoming the new (black) coffee, and paying homage to this new trend, Liverpool now has a number of trendy tea shops including Brew in St Paul's Square and Leaf on Parliament Street, both offering an impressive variety of teas from around the world and the ideal setting for putting the world to rights with a refreshing cuppa.

With everyone from fashion models to footballers' wives getting together to sip Earl Grey and munch on pastries, afternoon tea ha become quite the 21st century food fad.

Joining the tea party is celebrity hangout th St John Restaurant at the Sir Thomas Hotel, where you can nibble on assorted sandwiches tea time cakes, fresh baked scones with clotted cream and fruit preserves and sip freshly brewed tea from a selection – for a bit extra you can even add strawberries dipped in chocolate and a glass of Champagne.

Sue Kelbrick

CAFÉS

BREW TEA BAR
25 Bold Street
Liverpool L1 4DN
0151 708 7987
www.brewteabar.co.uk

As the name suggests they sell tea, lots of it and beautifully. As well as various loose teas, among them are a chocolate/chilli blend; Valentine's Tea and Fruit Punch. They also do tea lattes and tea smoothies and there's not a teabag in sight, everything is made from pure loose leaf brewed on Brew's unique conveyor belt order system before your eyes and using filtered water.

THE CHOCOLATE CELLAR
11-13 Hanover Street
Liverpool L1 3DN
0151 200 2202
www.thechocolatecellar.co.uk

Proprietor Bala Croman's tastebud-tingling chocolate creations have included rose and chilli, Moroccan mint and lime, pecan and cinnamon

and salt and pepper. As well as making truffles, cakes ar bars, The Chocolate Cellar offers a café with specialist chocolate drinks and workshops to learn about th art of chocolate making.

ACT CAFÉ
8 Wood Street
iverpool L1 4DQ
151 707 4450
ww.fact.co.uk
ıcked away on the ground ɔor of FACT, the bright and ry café aims to provide a ɔurce of nourishment for ɔth body and mind. Open om 8am Monday to Friday,).30am on Saturday and 1am on Sunday, the café ɜrves a delicious range of ·eakfasts, sandwiches, ılads and cakes – not to ıention some of the city's ıest speciality teas and ɔffees.

RATELLI CAFFE VERGNANO
3 Whitechapel
verpool
151 706 0074
ıis busy cosmopolitan café, ɜxt to Toni & Guy ıirdressers in Liverpool city ɜntre, is the place visiting ılians come to when they ant a decent cappuccino. un by the charming Antonio odica from Milan, it serves eat coffee and sandwiches, ısta dishes and salads.

LY ESPRESSAMENTE
aterstones
College Lane
verpool ONE L1 3DL
151 709 9820
ww.illy.com
y are widely regarded as ɔing the best coffee so ace that inside a huge ɔokshop in the middle of a ıstling shopping centre and ɔu are onto a winner. The ɜrfect place to hide away ɔm the crowds.

LEAF TEA SHOP AND BAR
27 Parliament Street
Liverpool L8 5RN
0151 707 7747
www.thisisleaf.co.uk
A 'punk tea shop' in the heart of Liverpool. Set on the ground floor of the freshly refurbished Elevator warehouse space, Leaf is a friendly café in the day with a delicious menu of scones, cakes and snacks, as well as more than 22 tea infusions from all over the world. For real tea aficionados – or those who'd like to be – there's a tea tasting master class. With good service, a superb wine list, and delicious food, it's one of a growing breed of places happy to serve you just drinks or drinks and food, calling itself a tea shop and wine bar. After dark, Leaf transforms itself into an alternative live music venue, showcasing DJs, bands, gallery space, films, art, knitting groups and anything else that takes their fancy.

THE MOCHA LOUNGE
Sir Thomas Street
Liverpool L1 6BA
0151 236 7737
This plush and palatial – but environmentally-conscious – coffee lounge, serves cakes

and pastries, light bites and alcohol, but it's still very much an oasis for coffee lovers to while away the hours. They have even introduced eco-friendly takeaway beakers made from corn, water and paper.

ROCOCO COFFEE HOUSE
Lord Street
Liverpool L2 6BP
0151 227 4822
www.rococoliverpool.com
It would be all too easy to miss this coffee shop, hiding up a flight of stairs on Lord Street. Rococo is about as sumptuous as coffee houses get with its opulent rococo styling, black and gold wallpapers, velvet sofas and chandeliers. As well as a good selection of coffees they also do hot chocolate and tea.

NIGHTLIFE

FROM the heady days of the Cavern, through the dance years at Cream, the Albert Dock's resurgence and now the ECHO arena and Liverpool ONE, this is a city that has always come alive after dark.

By day we are a thriving business city but it's at night, when Liverpool lets its hair down that the real magic begins.

Part of that comes from the fact that while there are distinct areas that come alive in the evenings, there is no real segregation within them. Uber-cool clubs sit alongside family restaurants, theatres nestle cheek by jowl with old fashioned ale houses.

A stone's throw from the rehearsal rooms The Zutons and The Wombats share with the city's up-and-coming unsigned acts lies Cains Brewery. A short stagger from the WAGtastic bars of Victoria Street lies Mathew Street, the top spot on the itineraries of the thousands of tourists who make the pilgrimage to get their pictures taken next to the Cavern Club, the place where it all began.

Liverpool is a small city, easily navigable on foot. In minutes you can stroll from the Pier Head to the Philharmonic Hall via the neoclassical splendours of St George's Hall, passing scores of venues on your way. The problem is choosing which to visit!

Jade Wright

LISTINGS

ALBERT DOCK

BLUE BAR & GRILL
Edward Pavilion
Liverpool L3 4AE
0151 702 5831
Head bartender Joanna Elkin serves Corona, Grey Goose Vodka & Cranberry Juice, and a deliciously zingy Mojito, but for a real treat, try the Jammie Dodger Shooter.

CIRCO
Britannia Pavilion
Liverpool L3 4AD
0151 709 0470
Part circus, part freakshow, it's the only venue in the city with a 10ft Polar Bear. Go along for their Freakshow nights, complete with fire eaters, stilt walkers, snake charmers and a host of other wonderful and weird things.

Clubbers let their hair down at Nation. Picture: Dangerous Disco

GUSTO
Edward Pavilion
Liverpool L3 4AF
0151 709 6969
Former tobacco warehouse Gusto is a Grade I listed building, which retains the original vaulted brick ceilings with stone floors. It can seat between 260-400, but the cosy intimate lighting and warm welcome makes it feel homely. The bar tender knocks up a fab English Bellini, Prosseco with pear puree and Manzana Verde, and the Mardi Gras is a riot of fruit flavours on a lemon base, Ketel One Citron vodka, fresh raspberries, fresh pressed apple juice and passion fruit.

PANAM
Britannia Pavilion
Liverpool L3 4AE
0151 702 5840
www.panam-venue.co.uk
Guests at PanAm can expect a diverse entertainment offering; those opting for a more relaxing evening can chill out in one of the intimate booths. Or, bring your dancing shoes and have fun to some of the regular live music on offer.

PORTICO CANTINA & BAR
Britannia Pavilion
Liverpool L3 4AD
0151 706 7400
www.porticocantina.co.uk
At the bar try the Shango Mojito, made with Bacardi, Velvet Falernum, fresh mint, sugar syrup and soda water, topped off with a Goslings Black Seal float. Shango is the Cuban God of Thunder and Debauchery, so the team at Portico thought it was only fitting to create a Mojito in his name. Legend has it, that anyone who consumes one of Shango's sacred Mojitos may one day possess his powers. Well, it's got to be worth a try...

TATE LIVERPOOL
Albert Dock
Liverpool L3 4BB
0151 702 7400
www.tate.org.uk
On the last Thursday of every month, Tate Liverpool opens its doors until 9pm for an evening of music, events, food and drink. Events have included the fabulous Night Fever, which saw the gallery transported to the 1970s with a silent disco dancefloor gallery space by Wayne Hemingway and his son Jack, and an arty party where fancy dress was a must.

VINEA
Britannia Pavilion
Liverpool L3 4AD
0151 707 8962
www.vinealiverpool.co.uk
Vinea is a real hidden gem. With good service, a superb wine list, and delicious food it's a specialist wine bar and shop, with big red and black sofas and paintings of pop culture icons dotted around Marilyn Monroe smiles down from one wall and a huge array of wine bottles on wooden shelves invite you to sample them. It's one of a growing breed of places happy to serve you just drinks or drinks and food, calling itself a wine bar, coffee bar and deli and staying open until 11pm most nights. If you're not sure what you want, or just fancy something new, their sommeliers are on hand to advise you.

Five fabulous cocktail bars

SANTA CHUPITOS
Devoted to the art of the cocktail, there's a huge black wall beside the bar listing the cocktails of the week – and there's nothing average at this relaxed and unpretentious Slater Street bar. Try the American Graffitti or Jamaican Me Stormy.

THE PLUM BAR, MALMAISON
The velvety surroundings make the perfect backdrop for a session sampling the cocktail menu here. The Mal knows how to knock up a classic Manhattan and the combination of Whiskey and Vermouth is guaranteed to keep you warm on cold winter nights.

RESTAURANT BAR & GRILL
The cocktail bar takes centre stage in the attractive eatery on Brunswick Street. We're big fans of the slick square bar and it's well equipped with numerous ingredients to attend our cocktail needs.

ALMA DE CUBA
It would be almost rude not indulge in a cocktail whilst visiting Alma De Cuba. The opulent settings of the former Polish church demand luxury in its many forms and where better to start than a cocktail? The only problem you'll have, is knowing where to start on the menu.

CHAMELEON BAR
When a joint offers a 'Bakewell Tartini' on the cocktail menu you have to, really, don't you? Chameleon shows that not all cocktail bars are the preserve of the sour puss and the socialite. This one's fun, too!

■ The Lemon Lounge
Picture: Dangerous Disco

HARDMAN STREET & HOPE STREET AREA

BAA BAR
7 Myrtle Street
Liverpool L7 7DN
0151 707 0610
www.baabar.co.uk
The new sister bar to the original Baa Bar in Concert Square. It bills itself as the best student bar in the world, with posh booths, a first floor clubspace, and a games room, plus great promo offers.

BAR HANNAH
2 Leece Street
Liverpool L1 2TR
0151 708 5959
Live music pours out of Bar Hannah – or Hannah's as it's more popularly known – drawing in a packed crowd of students and young professionals. Part New York, part Liverpool charm, the bar staff will fix you an array of cocktails to the back drop of bands or live DJs.

THE CASA
29 Hope Street
Liverpool L1 9BQ
0151 7092 148
About as far as you can get from your average chain bar, the Casa was bought by former Liverpool dockers who lost their jobs in the 90s. With a mixed bag of a clientele made up of students and many ex-dock workers themselves, the bar has a friendly atmosphere and a contemporary feel. As well as the bar, it offers two function rooms which host a variety of meetings for social groups in the area and gigs are held there too.

FLY IN THE LOAF
35 Hardman Street
Liverpool L1 9AS
0151 708 0817
Is there a more attractive pub frontage in Liverpool? This churchy-looking pub combines laid back charm in the day with a buzzing atmosphere by night. The beer is great, the service is quick and they do a Sunday roast to die for. Formerly Kirklands Wine Bar, and once upon a time a master bakery, it's a must-visit boozer at any time of day.

KOROVA
32 Hope Street
Liverpool L1 9BX
0151 709 7097
www.korova-liverpool.com
Whether you're calling in for a cheeky daytime pint, (and therefore will most probably end up staying for the surprisingly delicious noodles), or to watch live bands or big-screen football, Korova is the place to be. The atmosphere is laid back and welcoming, and the crowd, if a little on the 'youthful' side, are all gorgeous bright young things.

THE LEMON LOUNGE
21-23 Berry Street Liverpool L1 9DF
0151 709 5055
Setting up camp above the well-known Metropolitan Bar, The Lemon Lounge has styled itself into the birthplace of much of the house and dance music nights in this city. Offering a weekly showcase to big names along side some entrepreneurial youngsters makes this a special place. The drinks are reasonable, the crowd friendly and if you enjoy a rustic rave then this is without doubt the spot for you.

TRIBECA
15-19 Berry Street
Liverpool L1 9DF
0151 707 2528
Tribeca might give the appearance of a quiet, undiscovered bar and pizzeria. But fast forward past 11pm, and the mood changes – on comes the DJ, the diners clear out, and the crowds flood in. A relaxed, but unpretentious place to drink. 20 different types of rum are on offer, with 12 bourbons, six gins and 10 whiskies, along with 10 vodkas, thunder toffee and ultimate chocolate vanilla catching the eye.

LIVERPOOL ONE

LAS IGUANAS
14 Paradise Street
Liverpool L1 8JF
0151 709 4030
www.iguanas.co.uk
Latin rhythms playing in the background and an extensive choice of drinks – including caipirinha, Brazil's national drink. 2 for 1 on a selection of cocktails and pitchers during 'happy hour', 12pm – 7.30pm.

PALM SUGAR LOUNGE
5-6 Kenyon Steps
Liverpool ONE
0151 707 6654
www.palmsugarlounge.co.uk
As sweet as the name suggests, a decadent mix of far eastern culture and design with classic New York style cocktail bar action. The slick long running bar is like a runway from the main entrance, taking in bright colours and mirrored walls to create an aura of a space twice its size. On one side is the bar, staffed with an army of experienced shakers and makers – which means you're never left waiting for a drink. On the other, the floor to ceiling windows offer incredible views across the city's docks and waterfront. In warm weather, make the most of the alfresco seating area.

PIMA
Hilton Hotel
3 Thomas Steers Way
Liverpool ONE
0151 708 4200
www.hilton.co.uk/liverpool
The head barman at Pima in Liverpool's Hilton hotel, specialises in marvellous mojitos, beautiful Bellinis and cracking caipirinhas. Pima Prive is the intimate VIP area curtained off from the main bar – it needs to be booked, but it's like having your own mini night club – and comes with your very own cocktail waiter.

ZELIGS
8 Thomas Steers Way
Liverpool ONE
0151 709 7097
www.zeligs.co.uk
The brainchild of Rob Gutmann, the man behind Korova, Alma de Cuba, Circo and Raven. It's tucked deep in the foundations of the city's £1bn shopping development. There is no attempt to hide the giant concrete structure overhead and you can still see the spray-painted arrows which helped a legion of builders put Liverpool One together. It's also a music venue.

THE JAMES MONRO
69 Tithebarn Street
Liverpool L2 2EN
0151 236 9700
www.themonro.com

The James Monro on Tithebarn Street is named after the merchant vessel of the same name, which was the first ever scheduled passenger service from Liverpool to the Americas. It's a must for real ale fans – try the Sweet Chariot or one of their single cask malt whiskeys. Try cask number 1.4 from 1978 and enjoy a smooth, dreamy 32-year-old speciality.

THE LIVING ROOM
15 Victoria Street
Liverpool L1 6BD
0151 236 1999
www.thelivingroom.co.uk

Chic, upbeat and welcoming, with a guest list of celebrities other bars would die for. The club below the Living Room, Mosquito, used to be the famous SHE club. Try head bartender Zeljko Sunjar's fresh strawberries and basil muddled and then shaken with Gran Marnier, Chamborde and cranberry juice and finished with a hint of freshly ground black pepper.

MALMAISON
7 William Jessop Way
Liverpool
0151 229 5000
www.malmaison-liverpool.com

The Malmaison bar and brasserie has played host to Guy Ritchie, Gordon Ramsay, Westlife, Take That, Katie Price, Coleen Rooney and Alex Curran, Lulu, Anastacia, Jean Pierre Novelle, Marco Pierre White, Rhianna, Sugababes , Natasha Hamilton, Alisha Dixon, Kelly Brook and David Gest. Not that we're keeping count. It's slinky, sexy chic and stylish – a great place to pop into for a drink, including dreamy cocktails that change daily.

NEWZ BAR
18 Water Street
Liverpool L2 8TD
0151 236 2025
www.newzbar.co.uk

WAG hangout and celeb favourite Newz Bar has made a real name for itself in the city. The revamped Water Street venue attracts capacity crowds each weekend. Those who want to see and be seen line up at the mile-long marble bar, while those who are trying not to be seen party the night away in private booths. The restaurant upstairs, which doubles as a VIP area, sells bubbly by the box load at weekends, although the fridges are also well stocked with beer for every taste, and the cocktail menus are fully loaded with options.

NOBLE HOUSE
Heywood Building
5 Brunswick Street
Liverpool L2 0UU
0151 236 5346
www.thenoblehouse.co.uk

Noble House is set inside the famous Heywood building, fusing the discretion of a 1920s speakeasy with the style of a downtown Manhattan restaurant. The drinks are divine – ask head bartender Conor Foley to mix you a green apple martini – a tribute to the Big Apple itself or a breakfast martini, served with jam toast. After hours, indulge in a touch of underground glamour in the secret and discreet basement bar La Guarida and get yourself in a New York state of mind as you enjoy some of the best Martinis in the city.

CAVERN QUARTER

THE CAVERN
10 Mathew Street
Liverpool L2 6RE
0151 236 1965
www.cavernclub.org
Events include regular indie club/live music nights, unsigned bands and DJs from all over the UK. The Imagine Live nights are great club nights, live on the internet.

FLARES
8 Mathew Street
Liverpool L2 6RE
0151 255 0517
www.flaresbars.co.uk
The queue outside this place of a Saturday night is entertainment in itself: you'll find every size, shape and colour under the moon enjoying some lively banter with Liverpool as it passes by. Once inside, it's like Magaluf with a wig on. Perfect for pulling – pints or otherwise – Flares is the best Seventies-themed bar in the town and chockablock each weekend with stag and hen parties.

THE GRAPES
25 Mathew Street
Liverpool L2 6RE
0151 255 1525
You really ought to stop off for a pint in The Grapes. This is where the Fab Four drank in their Cavern-playing days. The evidence remains in a 1962 photograph taken of John, Paul, George and Pete Best, as they relaxed after one particular gig. You may even bump into their old promoter Sam Leech in the back room. Buy him a pint and he'll tell you all you ever wanted to know about Liverpool's most famous sons.

HARD DAYS NIGHT HOTEL
41 North John Street
Liverpool L2 6RR
0151 236 1964
Beatles fans will love the Hard Days Night hotel. It's a grade II listed Victorian building with a modern Beatles inspired twist. Bar Four does a superb Strawberry Fields cocktail – fresh strawberries crushed with lemon thyme herbs and sugar syrup, shaken with large measure of grass-infused vodka taken from the original site of Strawberry Fields and finished with a grind of fresh pepper.

THE WELKIN
7 Whitechapel
Liverpool L1 6DS
0151 243 1080
Wetherspoons' Welkin provides a wide variety of good cheap cask beer along with excellent quality, budget-conscious food. For the architecturally minded the pub is a treat too – one of those rare chrome and glass creations situated on the former site of the Philip Son & Nephew book store that is airy, spacious and pleasing to the eye. It certainly pulls in the punters and is one of the few licensed premises that opens at 9am for early breakfast.

THE WHITE STAR
2 Rainford Gardens
Liverpool L2 6PT
0151 231 6861
This former 19th century ships' chandlers is named after the great shipping company The White Star Line, and The Beatles were known to frequent the back room – just have a look at their nameplates on the chairs.

Deadmau5 wows the crowd at Cream's 17th Birthday Bash
Pictures by Dangerous Disco

Last night a DJ saved my life

IN days gone by, Liverpool's club scene was dominated by massive venues like Cream, Garlands and the 051.

But in recent years there's been something of a seismic shift in the city's nightlife as a new breed of smaller, cult club nights have emerged as real contenders.

The city's big players are still huge crowd pullers, as Garlands entertains countless glam-punters every weekend with its signature funky, vocal house and Cream's occasional nights at Nation are always a sell out.

But, rather than focusing on the venues, the emphasis is now firmly on individual nights by local promoters and DJs keen to experiment and bring world-renowned, credible DJs to the city.

Instrumental in giving Liverpool a reputation for a diverse and thriving club scene, these nights attract a knowledgeable, musically-aware crowd – and not the sort of people you're likely to see drunkenly dancing along to cheese and chart in Concert Square.

One of the biggest nights to emerge in the last few years is Circus, a tech, house and progressive dance night, which Cream resident, Yousef started in 2002 after the closure of Cream.

Circus's line-ups regularly feature the likes of Danny Howells, Paul Woolford and John Digweed; and its monthly parties at The Masque have become a not-to-be-missed part of any self-respecting Liverpudlian clubber's calendar.

Another huge club night is Chibuku Shake Shake, a house night with a distinctly studenty vibe, which started life in The Lemon Lounge on Berry Street in the late 90s before moving to The Masque on Seel Street.

Set in the upstairs part of The Metropolitan, The Lemon Lounge is a breeding ground for experimental, new club nights.

Freeze, Pigeonhole Disco and K Tuffle have all called this place home at one time or another, and you can always rely on this pint-sized venue to deliver a memorable night out.

Other not-to-be missed club nights include long-running house night, Igloo, Aztec and Freeze, which local lads Rab Casson and Andy Currie started as a house, tech house and progressive night in the Lemon Lounge and now hosts rave in a cave parties in the Williamson Tunnels every couple of months.

Also worth a visit is The Magnet – dark, dingy and with a somewhat sticky dance floor this Hardman Street venue is a place to go for those keen to entertain their ears with something different including deep house and techno night, VIVA VIDA.

Plus minimal, tech house and techno night, Coco De Mer, which generally holds events on the second weekend of the month.

The Magnet also regularly hosts the very-messy, very-late Circus and Chibuku after parties.

Despite being something of a mission to get to if you're walking from the city centre, The Picket, off Jamaica Street, also doesn't disappoint. The out-of-town venue is home to an eclectic line-up of warehouse parties, gigs and club nights, including electronic, house and techno night, MuMu and even hosted an unforgettable Circus after-party, which, according to local folklore, saw progressive legend, James Zabiela, play a blinder of a set alongside a giant dancing stuffed gorilla!

With the emphasis now firmly on individual nights rather than venues, posters, local clubbing sites like www.outlar.co.uk and local club forums, like www.circusclub.co.uk/forum are key to finding out when and where the best club nights in the city are happening.

Katie McLoughlin

ALMA DE CUBA
St Peter's Church
Seel Street
Liverpool L1 4BH
0151 702 7394
www.alma-de-cuba.com

Alma de Cuba is set inside the magnificent conversion of the former St Peter's Catholic Church and many of its ecclesiastical fittings still remain, including the original altar, stained glass windows and marble plaques. Renowned for its innovative cocktail list, favourites include Victoria's Secret – Wyborowa vodka, Giffard blackberry liqueur, Gilard wild strawberry liqueur, fresh strawberries, cranberry juice and black pepper – and Mai Tais Appleton VX rum, XM 5yr rum, Cointreau, Velvet Falernum, almond and pomegranate syrups, fresh orange, lime and pineapple juices.

CHAMELEON BAR
7-9 Back Colquitt Street
Liverpool L1 4NL
0151 707 0283
www.chameleonbar.co.uk

The Chameleon is cocktail heaven. Think a modern Alice in Wonderland, with Pete Clucas, manager and head bartender, at the centre of it all, mixing up his own imaginative cocktail menu. The Paris Hilton is by far the most popular. Made with fresh strawberry puree, home infused vanilla sugar and aged balsamic vinegar all mixed and reduced down together and then topped up with Venezuelan gold rum, fresh mint, strawberry liqueur and the final touch: pink Champagne.

HEEBIE JEEBIES
80-82 Seel Street
Liverpool L1 4BH
0151 708 7001

A nightlife institution, entirely in the good sense. It's lasted the test of time, partly down to its fab outside terrace bar for summer revellers. Live outdoor music and pitchers of cocktails seal the deal with this popular spot attracting a mixed crowd of students, post-work drinkers and pre-gig crowds.

LA'GO
20 Colquitt Street
Liverpool L1 4DE
0151 709 6116

La'go is in prime position on the corner of Seel Street and Colquitt Street. The bar itself is longer than in most places, meaning there's never much of a crush to get served. There are some seats and tables, room to stand, bits at both end where you can dance, and some toilets. But it works to keep it simple, in fact, if you look at the dodgy coloured glowing fireplaces they've installed, it's probably a good thing most of it is strictly no-frills.

LE BATEAU
Duke Street
Liverpool L1 5AA
0151 709 6508

Indiecation every Friday night at Le Bateau is always a good place for indie-kids to let loose on the dancefloor, in this nautical but nice nightclub, off the beaten track. Upstairs blasts out hands-in-the-air floorfillers whilst downstairs caters more for the connoisseurs of Indie and Electro music. Saturday nights are the legendary Liquidation, featuring dirty guitars and beats downstairs, and glam electro-punk upstairs.

THE MASQUE
90 Seel Street
Liverpool L1 4BH
0151 707 6171
www.masque-liverpool.com
Head down to The Masque for good drinks with good music and some very rock n roll cocktails – and to see the hottest new live bands. It's also home to club nights Circus and Chibuku. The downstairs bar Ink has a genuine traditional tattoo theme and the owners have spared no expense in transforming it into a real eye-catching, comfortable night out.

MELLO MELLO
40-42 Slater Street
Liverpool L1 4BX
0151 707 0898
Mello Mello is a gem of a gig venue. Part cafe, part bar, part venue it's run by an artistic collective, and as a result, the line-up is fairly alternative. Drop in for creative goings on, poetry readings and fabulous cake.

Irish eyes

THERE must be an official point where the Irish Sea starts and the Mersey ends - but, culturally at least, it's harder to locate – Liverpool even hosts its very own Irish Festival during October.

Accents and attitudes are similar, music and poetry flow through our veins. Peas in a pod. Or a stew, if you like.

As with the best traditional Irish bars, to enter the portals of the Pogue Mahone – which Shane MacGowan would be only too pleased to tell you means 'kiss my a***' in Gaelic – is to step into a separate dimension where all is languid like the gentle easy flow of the excellent draught Guinness; and the frenetic pace of normal modern life is locked outside on Seel Street with a bitterly cold wind for company.

Shenanigans on Tithebarn Street is always good craic too and serves one of the best pints of Guinness, not to mention the Emerald-isle style cocktails and shots such as the Irish Flag, Baby Guinness and Irish Whip. Reputedly the first bar in Liverpool to accept Euros as currency!

Set in the heart of Liverpool's nightlife on Mathew Street it would be easy for Flanagan's Apple to fall in with the rest of them but it has kept plenty of Irish tradition. This Irish pub has a real sense of character with a combination of great drinks, live bands and Irish music.

O'Neills is a popular and lively venue on the corner of Wood Street and Hanover Street, there's plenty of chance for a good old 'jig'. As well as serving a great range of drinks such as Irish themed cocktails, Caffrey's, Smithwick's, Magners and Guinness you can also try a selection of Irish dishes from their Taste of Ireland menu, which includes Irish stew crock pot with Irish soda bread or Limerick ham and Irish cheddar quiche.

And remember you don't have to be Irish to get a welcome in the parlour – just leave the stupid leprechaun hat at home, okay?

MODO
Concert Square
Liverpool L1 4AR
0151 709 8832
This trendy late bar, with two floors, three bars and a chill-out area, is a big hit with students and young professionals. There are also plenty of nooks and crannies with leather sofas to lounge on and have a chat. The DJ tucked away at the back of the bar plays uplifting funky dance on most evenings. One of the best places in Liverpool to start and end a night, as there never seems any rush to move on.

MOOD
18-20 Fleet Street
Liverpool L1 4AN
0151 709 8181
With three floors and five rooms, Mood is the superclub that never seems to sleep. As one of the largest bars in the city Mood stands tall commanding a great view along Fleet Street. This is a sure fire hit with the city's younger, party crowd.

MOJO
Back Berry Street
Liverpool L1 4BG
0151 707 0828
www.mojobar.co.uk
A rock and roll cocktail bar. Their ethos is to get as rich a mixture of people in as possible, from 21 to 65, so there's a relaxed dress and door policy. Like its sister bars in Leeds and Manchester, Liverpool's Mojo sticks to doing what it knows, and doing it well, so you won't find food, alcopops, draught beer or bands with dodgy sound systems here. What you do get is carefully chosen classic rock, a connoisseur's selection of liquors and beer served ice-cold.

NATION
Wolstenholme Square
Liverpool L1 4BX
For a night to remember, head to clubbing Mecca Nation. Presided over by Penelope, a massive twisted organic looking piece of Jorge Pardo public art, it has been home to Cream, Medication and Chibuku nights, among many, many others.
Inside it's an Alice in Wonderland of a club, with dancing spread over three rooms, each of varying shape and size.
The visuals and lighting system are great, and logos spin and slide across the dark walls. It holds thousands, but don't let that fool you, there's normally a queue outside, especially for the more popular events.

PARR STREET STUDIOS
33-45 Parr Street
Liverpool L1 4JN
0151 707 1050
www.parrstreet.co.uk
Parr Street is a hub for Liverpool's music scene, and the biggest studio in the country outside London. Try 33-45 upstairs, for drinks and dancing, or downstairs, Studio2 is a breakfast bar in the morning, an events venue by day and a haven for music-loving drinkers at night.

THE PEACOCK
49-51 Seel Street
Liverpool L1 4AZ
0151 709 5052
Pleasantly brimming with a varied crowd, this trendy pub is known for its superb music. Instead of tedious repetition of the same Sixties records or dreaded Scouse-house, you will hear a varied selection of new indie, proper rock 'n' roll and electronica. A bustling little cocktail menu, some interesting beers and a smoking terrace with heaters – what more could you want?

The university of life

LIVERPOOL is one of the best university cities in the country and it's not hard to see why.

With three excellent universities in John Moore's, Hope and Liverpool University itself, each have excellent student unions which put on a variety of nights.

But it's Liverpool's fantastic and varied city centric nightlife that really attracts the more social students to the city, and one of the major reasons that it has built a great reputation as a great place to play as well as study.

Liverpool during the week really belongs to students and there is something to do every night Monday to Thursday. The Razz or Blue Angel, is full most nights of the week but there is also Cheeky Monkey at Mood on a Monday, Tuesday is Mischief, Wednesday is the legendary Medication at Nation, Thursday is Vodka Nation at Garlands – and surrounding these big club nights there is a myriad of bars enticing in the student pound! At the weekends students tend to do their own thing but usually bar hop around the city centre, enjoying watering holes such as The Cambridge, The Flute, the new Baa Bar, Bar Hannah, Bar Ca Va, Revolution and Camel Club on Wood Street.

If you like your music electronic, Annie Mac-style, Chibuku is fortnightly at the Masque and always has great acts on and a loyal following.

Other great places to end a night include The Krazy House on Wood Street, Mixed Bag @ Masque, and Le Bateau.

When money is tight, you can probably have a good night out for 20 quid which includes entrance into a club, a few drinks, a pizza or kebab and at the end of the night your cab home (which are always easy to get midweek!)

Liverpool – the University of Life. Your further education starts here!

Marc Jones

GAY LIVERPOOL

The Homotopia float hits the sunny city streets for The Lord Mayor's Parade

LIVERPOOL already wows the North West with Homotopia and the Outsiders Film Festival, but the city's first Liverpool Pride since the 1990s will make 2010 a year for special celebration.

Tommy McIlravey, of Liverpool Pride said: "On August 7, we want the whole city to know what's going on, we want to march down Liverpool's busy streets and make a visible statement that the LGBT community are here, contribute and have rights too. We want Liverpool Pride to be for everyone, to bridge the gaps between communities and bring people together."

Like the rest of the city, Liverpool's Gay Quarter has seen massive investment in recent years. Most venues are found around Stanley Street, Cumberland Street, Victoria Street and Eberle Street - in the heart of the city centre. The scene has a varied mix of bars and clubs with something to suit everyone's taste. The Lisbon, the Curzon and the Masquerade are the old die-hards, each offering something different from the next. The Lisbon, a favourite meeting point, is renowned for its ornate ceiling inside. Known locally as 'the Lizzie', you'll see most of Liverpool's scene queens here at some point, shooting pool, or flaunting their stuff on the dancefloor. The Masquerade, billed as 'Liverpool's friendliest gay bar' is also another adored drinking hole on the scene, and home to two of Liverpool's best-known drag and cabaret acts Aunty Marlene and Doreen Kumkwik. G-Bar, on Eberle Street, is perhaps the busiest after hours club on the gay scene and opens until silly o'clock at weekends. Across the road is Garlands - Liverpool's original gay superclub. From the tacky to the trendy, the loud to the laid back, Liverpool's gay scene has it all.

Richie Wright

www.liverpoolgayscene.com

LISTINGS

BAR CANDY
8-10 Stanley Street
Liverpool L1 6AF
Open Thursdays to Sundays, Bar Candy lets you party like a rock star to everything from funky house, dance, diva classics, to your favourite cheesy pop.

THE CURZON
8 Temple Lane
Liverpool L2 5RQ
0151 236 5160
One of Liverpool's oldest gay bars and probably the most male-dominated. Events include a monthly fetish night called LADS.

DESTINATION
21 Temple Street
Liverpool L2 5RH
Exclusively gay owned and run, this place delivers a great atmosphere with a strict door policy. Themed parties, live PAs, and fabulous cabaret, this club has fast become the destination to be.

Loud and proud at G-Bar

GARLANDS
8-10 Eberle Street
Liverpool L2 2AG
0151 231 1105
Named in honour of the iconic Judy Garland, this glamorous club attracts clubbers of all persuasion from far and wide. Award-winning and with its own twin in Ibiza, Garlands has been setting trends in club land since day one. The crowd is more mixed than predominantly gay, with an array of ages and costumes, from trendy young things to pop princesses. Famous for outrageous themed shows, over-dressed drag queens and boat parties on the river Mersey.

G-BAR
1-3 Eberle Street
Liverpool L2 2AG
0151 236 4416
Voted Liverpool Club of the Year by the Liverpool Echo in 2008 and voted into the top five after-hours venues in Britain by world-famous Mixmag, the G-Bar is legendary on the Liverpool scene. Split into three rooms; the famous Church Room, complete with church alters and décor to boot; the Basement, a den of sin and thumping DJ beats; and the Piano Lounge, a haven where clubbers can relax.

HEAVEN
3 Victoria Street
Liverpool L2 2QA
0151 236 4832
A hands-in-the-air paradise, with two rooms – a bar and a club – Heaven brings the biggest parties, DJs and PAs to Victoria Street.

JUPITERS
10 Hackins Hey
Liverpool L2 2AW
0151 227 5265
A welcoming bar on the edge of Liverpool's Gay Quarter. The bar is spread over two floors and attracts a mixed crowd particularly popular with the lesbian community. Popular nights are Thursgays and Sungays – no explanation needed for which night of the week they are on!

THE LISBON
35 Victoria Street
Liverpool L1 6BG
0151 231 6831
A vast and traditionally-styled location with an intricate ceiling above a spacious bar, complete with tables and comfortable snugs. During the day, you can order from a menu of pub fayre or play a game of pool. While, later in the evening, the diverse crowd and mix of non-stop party tunes ensures that the dancing starts very early on in this busy meeting place!

THE MASQUERADE
10 Cumberland Street
Liverpool L1 6BU
0151 236 7786
The Mazzie is a small bar with a big heart. There's no room for wallflowers here, with DJs and drag queen hostesses determined to make your night one to remember. The mixed crowd has the shared objective of having a good time, and this popular cabaret bar is the life and soul of the party throughout the week.

Superstar Boudoir

NAVY BAR
27-29 Stanley Street
Liverpool L1 6AA
You'll be hard pushed to find a space on the dance floor and podiums here, amongst the loved-up crowd, surrendering to the best tunes in clubland.

PINK
4-6 Victoria Street
Liverpool L2 6QE
No prizes for guessing what colour this bar is – a hit with gay people and their friends.

THE POSTE HOUSE
23 Cumberland Street
Liverpool L1 6BU
0151 236 4130
Renowned for cheap spirits and shots, this place is popular with the younger crowd who cram the upstairs bar most nights of the week.

PUZZLE
25 Stanley Street
Liverpool L1 6AA
Set in the former Bar Du Fay, Puzzle offers cheap drinks, great DJs, and two floors for dancing or chilling out. The first Saturday of every month is Girls Go Down, a fabulous night for ladies, wherever you sit on the rainbow.

STRAY
9 Victoria Street
Liverpool L2 5QA
Stray is a vibrant gay club located on the former site of H Bar. The venue is spread over two floors and offers DJs, live entertainment and a great range of drinks including cocktails.

SUPERSTAR BOUDOIR
22-24 Stanley Street
Liverpool L1 6AF
The place where people of all persuasions come to party. You can't miss the drag hostess at the door, who sets the tempo for a night of glamour. You can head to the main room for dancing, or relax in the low-key lounge to chat with friends. A friendly mix of beautiful young things.

FESTIVALS

LIVERPOOL PRIDE

www.liverpoolpride.co.uk

The city's first Liverpool Pride since the 1990s takes place on August 7, 2010 with the theme 'Rainbow Circus'. At the time of writing, plans were afoot for a Pride march starting from St George's plateau at midday and taking in Liverpool's Gay Quarter and parts of the city centre. The Dale Street area will be closed off until 8pm for the Pride street party with music, cabaret and street entertainers embracing the rainbow circus theme, before a big finale. A number of Pride arts and sports events will be taking place on Sunday, August 8, with Liverpool City Council actively encouraging organisations and groups to get involved.

A warm welcome at the launch of Homotopia

HOMOTOPIA

www.homotopia.net

Every year in November, the city hosts Homotopia, a two-week festival of gay culture including theatre, film, photography, and art. Launched in 2004, and supported by the Arts Council England, the celebration has now become a highlight of Liverpool's cultural calendar. In contrast to a traditional 'Pride' festival, Homotopia is a forum to showcase LGBT talent in the field of arts, photography and performance, and is designed to bring together creative individuals irrespective of sexuality. Shows and events take place in theatres and galleries around Liverpool, and tend to be separate from the traditional gay scene. The opening and closing ceremonies do, however, often involve some form of club night! Homotopia has been attended by numerous high profile figures from international gay society, including Peter Tatchell, Holly Johnson, Armistead Maupin and Amy Lame. Homotopia also represents the gay community with its own float in Liverpool's annual Lord Mayor's Parade, along with other communities in the city.

OUTSIDERS FILM FESTIVAL

www.outsidersfilmfestival.com

This LGBT film festival brings the latest in gay film to the city. Outsiders holds monthly film screenings all year round at FACT, as well as hosting a two week bumper festival every October. Guests to previous festivals have included gay rights campaigner Larry Kramer, Roz Kaveney, Simon Callow, Rose Troche, David Paisley, Christopher Hobbs and the legendary Rosa von Praunheim. Patrons include Chris Bernard (director of Letter to Brezhnev), the singer Thomas Lang and the actor Sir Derek Jacobi KBE.

The Ship & Mitre on Dale Stree

MINE'S A PINT!

YOU can't beat a good pint – and you can't beat drinking it in a good pub. Which means we're extremely lucky in Liverpool: the Capital of Pubs and Capital of Real Ale.

The city has rolled out the barrel with much to discover on the real ale trail.

Our historic, flagship brewery, Cains – the Stanhope Street site was acquired by Irish entrepreneur Robert Cain in 1858 – represents the beating heart of the city's pub life. After an uncertain period in the latter part of the 20th century, it was placed firmly back on the map when it was taken over by Ajmail and Sudarghara Dusanj in 2002.

Beer festivals are held – and well-supported – here, there and everywhere. Underpinning everything, with their ceaseless support of the local pub scene, is the Liverpool and District branch of CAMRA (Campaign for Real Ale) – volunteers who devote so much of their time and effort to flying the flag not just for Liverpool's pubs, but the city itself.

Here in Liverpool we have an unrivalle combination of great pubs with great choice and quality of real ale. You can los yourself in a good pub – restore your spirit and restore your sanity (while, obviously, refuelling at the same time). Adopted Scouser and former Liverpool player Jan Molby once summed up the spirit of life in Liverpool when he said: "When it's Tuesday night and you're out having a bevvy, no one's thinking about Wednesday morning".

We are well-blessed with terrific, traditional pubs. Yes, we have some of the best locals in the country – and some of the best beer. And there is quantity as well as quality. To be honest, it's impossible to devise a single pub crawl which would give a drinker the ultimate Liverpool pub experience. There are so many boozers worthy of our time and attention, including many on the outskirts and in the suburbs, that it could take days – weeks, even – to get around the very best this well-blessed area has to offer.

But, if you can manage taking in these city centre pubs in a day, or over a weekend (perhaps a half in each, or the odd soft drink!) I don't think you could go wrong with the following route.

There can be no better place to start a pub crawl through Liverpool than the boozer which sits just a few yards from Cains brewery.

If the various pints of various award-winning Cains ales are not going to taste like nectar in **The Brewery Tap** on Upper Stanhope Street, they're not going to anywhere. Thankfully, the major made-in-Liverpool brews always seem to be in tip-top condition at the terrific Tap.

The only downside to this drinker's delight is its location, but don't panic, it really isn't at the end of the earth – a short taxi ride will do it, and, once you have, you are more likely to savour your session.

After a quick stop at the wonder of Wapping – **The Baltic Fleet** – we're off towards the city centre's business district, to **Ma Boyle's Oyster Bar**, snugly tucked away in Tower Gardens next to Liverpool Parish Church (aka St Nick's). This happy haven is still noted for its home-cooked food, not least its Scouse and famous fish dishes.

The Cornmarket is one of Liverpool's oldest boozers and one of its biggest – almost hidden away in The Old Ropery, off Fenwick Street. It may give the impression that it's on the smallish size, but this Tardis-like boozer seems to go on for miles inside and includes a heated beer garden, accessible from the right-hand side of the bar.

The Slaughterhouse, in Fenwick Street, is one of our oldest pubs – and it's also said to be one of our most haunted alehouses. In fact, one ex-landlord said that he was so spooked by the place he would never lock up at night alone. But when it's open, you'd rarely be alone in this thriving, atmospheric boozer.

On and just off Dale Street, you'll find Thomas Rigby's and its accompanying bar The Lady of Mann, The Saddle Inn and Ye Hole In Ye Wall – hardly any crawling required here at all!

Thomas Rigby's, a real old city favourite, is mighty in size and mighty in reputation. There's a different atmosphere in each of the pub's three rooms: the large, main bar; the Nelson

room at the back of the building (well, he is supposed to have popped in for a pint once) and the relaxed parlour on the right-hand side of the pub. Behind Rigby's, beyond the boozer's courtyard drinking area, is **The Lady of Mann**.

At first sight, especially on a run-of-the-mill weekday lunchtime, Rigby's next door neighbour **The Saddle Inn** may seem a typically traditional and understated city boozer, but this long-standing favourite attracts a wide range of customers at different times.

The Guinness is impressive and, with its good value, home-cooked food, it's a pub that fits in well in the business district on weekdays. A few feet away, up Hackins Hey, is **Ye Hole In Ye Wall**, which is a real, best-of-both-worlds oasis – yes, it's in the heart of the city, but it's nicely tucked away up a tiny side street.

Ye Hole, which claims to be the oldest pub in the city (it's not the only one!), boasts attractive dark wood panelling, leather seating, stained glass windows and comfortable side rooms tucked away from the main bar.

The Lion Tavern, at the corner of Moorfields and Tithebarn Street, continues to ply its ever-popular trade in real ales, specialist malt whiskies and specialist, locally-sourced food – watch out for its famous cheese board and award-winning pork pies. The Lion Tavern packs plenty of class into three rooms; including a glass dome, exquisite tile work and wonderful wooden panelling.

This was one of Robert Cain's Victorian gems and, as such, it is the final word in craft, culture and quality – that etched and stained glass obviously took time and loving care to create.

The Poste House, in nearby Cumberland Street, dates back to 1820. Noted for its nicely priced real ale and spirits, cosiness and friendly atmosphere, it's one of the few pubs which has actually improved after undergoing a mini-refurb. It's a cracking little pub – central and yet, situated on a side street between Dale Street and Victoria Street, away from the crowds.

Back onto Dale Street – its very edge, close to the tunnel end – and **The Ship and Mitre** has long been held up to be Real Ale Central by beer lovers.

The Lion Tavern

One of the few remaining Art Deco buildings left in the city centre, the pub has up to 12 real ales on at any one time. It is also justifiably proud of its range of ciders, imported lagers and wheat beers – and the eight beer festivals it stages during the year.

Doctor Duncan's

Doctor Duncan's, in St John's Lane, is another landmark Liverpool pub – and another architectural gem. It has the look and feel of a pub which has been around for decades, but this real tonic of a boozer only opened for business as recently as 1999. It's not easy to find a seat in there – but when you do, sit back and savour your sensational surroundings, especially if you sit in its handsome bar, and look out over St John's Gardens.

Ma Egerton's, aka Ma E's, on the corner of Pudsey Street and Lord Nelson Street near Lime Street Station, has an olde worlde atmosphere which is reinforced by the old time live entertainment it provides and its theatrical connections (it's within spitting distance of the Empire Theatre, but don't spit – because it's not nice).

If **The Grapes**, in Mathew Street and **The White Star**, in Rainford Gardens just around the corner, were good enough for the Beatles (who, I reckon, concentrated too much on their music, at the expense of the ale), then they're good enough for us. These city favourites have been at the top of the popularity charts for years, and probably would be even if they were situated well away from Cavernland.

The Beehive in Paradise Street is one of far-too-few pubs to be found smack bang in the middle of Shopping Central and has always been a welcoming haven for shoppers who are tired of scurrying, and yearn to start supping.

A short walk away, in Tarleton Street, there is another great shopping centre survivor – **The Carnarvon Castle,** which opened in the 1880s, at one time shared the street with seven other boozers. Not much more crawling is required to reach **The Richmond** in Williamson Street, by Williamson Square. It's a smallish boozer and the ale choice includes the delicious Deuchars IPA, Black Sheep bitter, Cains bitter and Bass bitter.

The Globe in Cases Street is one of the great pubs in Liverpool city centre – and the world! This gem of a place offers a friendly service, a friendly atmosphere generated by its friendly staff and customers, a relaxing back room, well-kept real ales . . . and standing by the large window at the front of the pub is a great place to watch the world rush by outside.

And so onto the force of nature that is the mighty **Swan Inn**, in Wood Street. The Swan is loud (owing to its thunderously good, heavy-duty jukebox), proud but also laid-back, thanks to its "take us as you find us" attitude and atmosphere.

The Dispensary, another city centre 'local', sits on the corner of Renshaw Street and Oldham Street, just yards from the busy Bold Street, Berry Street, Leece Street/Hardman Street interchange. It provides a warm and friendly drinking environment, great service and great Cains ales.

An altogether different pub – variety is the spice of life in the Liverpool drinking scene – is the **Roscoe Head**, in Roscoe Street, one of only 10 pubs in the country to appear in every edition of the Good Beer Guide.

Some pubs simply can't fail to impress, such is their pedigree. **The Fly In The Loaf**, on Hardman Street, for example, boasts a striking exterior, a striking (it goes on for miles) interior and some strikingly good real ales. Oh, and in 2007 it was named the best pub in Britain by listeners to Radio Five Live. That, you must agree, is pretty impressive.

The Philharmonic in Hope Street is a huge and hugely popular pleasure palace. It was commissioned by Robert Cain, and it was designed and built by brewery architect Walter W. Thomas, between 1898 and 1900.

Walk in and around this architectural masterpiece and absorb its treasures – the mosaic floor, mahogany panels, stained glass, intricate carvings, the Grande Lounge with its chandeliers and leather furniture and so much else of beauty and sublime craftsmanship. Time appears to stand still in **Ye Cracke**, on Rice Street, a unique Liverpool pub which resolutely remains the same year after year after year.

It is the antithesis of anything and everything that is new, shiny, glitzy, glam posh and pretentious – the Cracke just gets on with doing what it does best . . . providing a casual, comfortable haven for those who are really not that bothered about keeping pace with the fads and fashions of modern life. Yet another Tardis-like Liverpool pub, it boasts (wait for it) . . . a small bar at the front, a back room leading to a beer garden (great view of Liverpool Cathedral in one corner), a main bar and adjacent seating area, complete with murals on the walls, and a quiet side room known as The War Office.

Just down the hill, **The Pilgrim** is another laid-back pub which effortlessly makes its customers feel at ease. And it always helps a pub's cause when the drinking is done below street level –

The Philharmonic

urther removed from the everyday bustle ·f the city outside. The Pilgrim's drinking ·ooths also add to the atmosphere, as does ts attractive brickwork – yes, it's very asy to walk down the stairs and into the 'ilgrim's comforting arms, but it's not lways easy to leave.

The Belvedere on Sugnall Street just ff Falkner Street, may be small in size, ·ut it's big on atmosphere and appeal. A mall and charming Victorian Grade II isted building, The Belvedere is easy to niss and yet is situated in an excellent pot in the heart of Liverpool's Georgian uarter.

The Grapes on Knight Street (known s the "Little Grapes") is housed in a ery old building and benefits from its ld-fashioned values – which, as well as he good service, also include ensuring the eer is top-notch and that there's an asy-going, relaxed atmosphere. These, of course, are big and important things, whatever the size of the boozer.

The Crown on Lime Street is, due to its location, one of the first and last boozers people experience when they arrive in/leave Liverpool by rail. And it should leave them with good memories, because it's a traditional, no-nonsense pub which has a large, open-plan lounge and a good-sized back lounge, from where you can happily stare at those poor souls dashing to Lime Street station, safe in the knowledge you have no plans to go any further than the bar for another pint.

Is that enough crawling around Liverpool city centre? No, not really, it just represents the tip of an enormous iceberg. It's a journey – or crawl – which will no doubt lead to you discovering other places along the way. Cheers!

Paddy Shennan

PULLING POWER

TAKING place in mid-February, the Liverpool Real Ale Festival enjoyed its 30th anniversary in 2010 and continues to grow in popularity amongst traditionalists and a growing younger audience.

Offering a choice of over 250 real ales, ciders, perrys and fruit wines, the volunteer-run event is housed in The Crypt of Liverpool Metropolitan Cathedral. Indeed, it is the only cathedral in the world to house such an event. Although a bigger venue has been touted given the increasing difficulty in purchasing tickets, the conditions of the location for storage mean that the ales can be kept at a premium temperature, retaining quality and flavour. In short – organisers, quite rightly, do not want to compromise the quality of the product.

Members of the Campaign For Real Ale (CAMRA) are usually given priority for tickets. The rest are made available for the general public at the cathedral (The Gibberd Room in

The micro-brewery at the Baltic Fleet

The Liverpool Real Ale Festival

ecent years), usually on the morning of the rst Saturday in December. However, it's ecommended to get there at worst an hour efore opening to guarantee tickets.

In December 2009 ahead of the 2010 estival, customers could only buy four tickets when in previous years it's been up to 12 ckets – including a maximum of four for the riday night.

The festival itself is spread over three days, aking in a five-hour Thursday evening ession; and afternoon and evening four-hour penings on the Friday and Saturday. Priced at 6 each in 2010, tickets guarantee you dmission.

Once inside you pay £10 for beer vouchers – nd a customary festival glass and rogramme – with vouchers marked once you egin ordering, depending on the cost of the easure you'll have purchased.

There are plenty of seating areas available to park yourself, and a stage from which live music is provided (excluding Friday afternoon).

As the session progresses the warm, friendly atmosphere becomes more lively – but always civil! The festival also continues to gain in popularity with ladies, with female-only guests also invited to taste the product on the eve of the festival.

For those seeking a taste of something local during the rest of the year, you could do worse than try the Ship and Mitre (113 Dale Street), which hosts regular mini-festivals, usually consisting of ale, European lagers and ciders.

The Baltic Fleet (33 Wapping), a fine Grade II-listed edifice situated near the Albert Dock, even has its own micro-brewery and is another jewel in the crown of Liverpool pubs.

James Cleary

For more info visit: www.merseycamra.org.uk

SPORT

ANFIELD is instantly recognisable as the home to Liverpool Football Club.

Liverpool's magnificent trophy haul includes 18 league championships, five European Cups and seven FA Cups. The scale of the club's achievements and the legends that have played at Anfield attracts fans from all over the world, who pack out the stadium on matchdays.

The pull of the Kop, the most atmospheric stand in world football, is an irresistible draw, although tickets for Liverpool matches are notoriously difficult to come by. A capacity of 45,362 is nowhere near enough to satisfy demand and the club is planning to relocate to a new stadium to be built in nearby Stanley Park.

While the football season runs between August and May, Anfield is open to visitors all year round. The club store is full of all manner of memorabilia (there are two more in the city centre), while the stadium tour takes people behind the

scenes, allowing you to get a real feel for what makes the place so special.

You can sit in the dressing room where the likes of Steven Gerrard and Fernando Torres compose themselves before every home match. You can even touch the 'This Is Anfield' sign for good luck before making your way down the tunnel and out towards the pitch.

The club's museum enables visitors to walk through the club's unparalleled history, from the beginnings in the late 19th century to the successes of recent years. Among the items you can marvel at is the European Cup trophy awarded to Liverpool after the astonishing win over AC Milan in 2005. There is an eight-foot bronze statue of legendary manager Bill Shankly outside the club shop that depicts the inspirational Scot with his arms outstretched and a fan's scarf around his neck.

Outside the ground, on Anfield Road, is the Hillsborough memorial. Featuring an eternal flame, it contains the names and ages of the 96 Liverpool supporters who lost their lives at the FA Cup semi-final on April 15 1989.

All this makes up Anfield, but it's worth remembering that the stadium existed before Liverpool FC was formed, as it was originally the home of the other major football club in the city – Everton.

Although they tend to be overshadowed by their more glamorous neighbours, Everton are a great club in their own right. Formed in 1878, Everton were based at Anfield from 1884 to 1892 when a dispute with the club chairman and Anfield owner, John Houlding, led to Everton's board of directors walking out.

Houlding formed a new club, calling them Liverpool, and an intense rivalry was born. It is 25 years since the Blues' greatest season when the Everton of 1984/85 won the league championship, European Cup Winners' Cup and reached the FA Cup final. In total, they've amassed nine league titles and five FA Cups. The arrival of David Moyes as manager in 2002 heralded a revival and Everton have become established as the most consistent Premiership team outside the financial heavyweights of Manchester United, Chelsea, Arsenal and Liverpool.

There are two club stores selling official merchandise: 'Everton One' is situated opposite Goodison Park while 'Everton Two' is based in the 'Liverpool ONE' shopping complex (see what they've done there?) Attendances for matches tend to be between 35,000 and 40,000, with tickets almost always available through general sale. Evertonians are very attached to their 40,157-capacity stadium, which is an old-fashioned ground and can be intimidating to opposition teams when the fans are in full voice.

A focal point for Evertonians is the Dixie Dean statue situated outside the Park End stand. This was erected in tribute to the club's greatest player, a striker who scored an astonishing 383 goals in 433 Everton appearances. His record of scoring 60 league goals in a single season, 1927/28, will surely never be broken.

Alan Jewell

RACING

AINTREE RACECOURSE
Ormskirk Road
Aintree L9 5AS
0151 523 2600
www.aintree.co.uk

Venue of the John Smith's Grand National – four miles and 856 yards that have 600 million viewers glued to their television sets all over the globe. The views over Aintree Racecourse are among the finest in world sport. The venue has had £35m lavished on it in recent years, work which saw Aintree transformed from a ramshackle collection of buildings held together by flaking paint into a blueprint for the future of world-class sports facilities. Two new grandstands, the Lord Sefton and the Earl Of Derby, were opened to great acclaim in 2007, while the new parade ring, winner's circle and weighing room complex came on stream the year before. The Saturday of the John Smith's Grand National has excitement and anticipation in abundance as the build-up develops towards the big race. Ladies' Day at Aintree is the fastest-selling day at the John Smith's Grand National meeting and is undeniably the social highlight in the North West of England, with style the order of the day. There is superb racing on the Thursday opening day of the John Smith's Grand National meeting, which is more relaxed than the Friday and the Saturday – but just as enjoyable. When it's not home to the most famous race in the world, Aintree plays host to an additional six race days, incorporating entertainment, music and of course, racing.

CHESTER RACECOURSE
The Roodee
Chester CH1 2LY
01244 304600
www.chester-races.co.uk

With racing on the site dating back to 1539, Chester is the oldest racecourse in Britain, and possibly the world. Racing begins with a three-day May festival, putting Chester in the racing spotlight nationally. This festival has long been the flagship fixture, providing the very highest level of racing, the chance to see some of the best-known names in the sport and permeating throughout, an unquestionably fun atmosphere! After May, there are another 10 days and evenings of racing throughout the summer months. Each fixture has its own unique identity to ensure a wide-ranging appeal, starting with the May Festival and then moving onto the Ladies' evenings, Roman Day and Family Funday amongst much more

HAYDOCK PARK RACECOURSE
Newton-le-Willows WA12 0HQ
01942 725 963
www.haydock-park.co.uk

Over 250 years old and one of the country's premier racecourses. An exciting programme of events is offered throughout the year, with 32 racedays featured in 2010, all set in 127 acres of beautiful parkland.

TENNIS

LIVERPOOL INTERNATIONAL TENNIS TOURNAMENT
Calderstones Park, Childwall
Liverpool L18 3JD
www.liverpooltennis.co.uk

As one of the key warm-ups to Wimbledon the Tradition-ICAP Liverpool International is a must in the calendar for ATP and WTA players. Since its inception in 2002, the event has seen crowds thrilled by stars such as Martina Navratilova, Bjorn Borg, Goran Ivanisevic, Pat Cash, Martina Hingis, Henri Leconte, Xavier Malisse and David Ferrer. In June 2010, legend John McEnroe will join that list.

.IFESTYLES TENNIS CENTRE
11 Wellington Road
Vavertree L15 4LE
)151 293 8350
www.liverpool.gov.uk
'his 'Centre of Excellence' for ennis features six indoor ınd outdoor courts, as well ıs a full range of coaching rom mini tennis for children ıp to those now playing at ıational level.

CRICKET

.IVERPOOL CRICKET CLUB
\igburth Road
Grassendale L19 3QF
)151 427 2930
www.liverpoolcricketclub.co.uk
Founded in 1807, Liverpool Cricket Club stages Lancashire first-team games on the top pitch and over the years has played host to some of the world's greatest cricketers – WG Grace and Wasim Akram have all been mpressed by the standard of facilities here.

RUGBY

ST HELENS RUGBY LEAGUE
GPW Recruitment Stadium
Dunriding Lane
St Helens WA10 4AD
www.saintsrlfc.com
One of the country's greatest rugby league teams, Saints play in the engage Super League and have most recently won the Carnegie Challenge Cup Trophy three years in a row and the League Leaders' Shield for four consecutive years. The club will move into their new stadium in 2011.

SWIMMING

LIVERPOOL AQUATICS CENTRE
Wellington Road
Liverpool L15 4LE
0151 233 8850
www.liverpool.gov.uk
The state-of-the-art £17m facility in Wavertree has an Olympic-sized 50m pool with a moveable floor. It also houses a 400-seat athletics arena and can host major championships.

DUNES SPLASH WORLD
The Esplanade
Southport PR8 1RX
01704 537160
www.splashworldsouthport.com
All-weather leisure pool with tube ride, four-lane slide, river, water curtains, fountain and water cannon.

CLIMBING

AWESOME WALLS
St Albans Church
Athol Street
Liverpool L5 9XT
0151 298 2422
www.awesomewalls.co.uk
Lead climb to the rafters, or stand watching in the aisles with a cup of tea. Experience is not an issue at AWCC as there are beginner courses available that teach you the ropes (no pun intended).

EXTREME SPORTS

THE HUB FESTIVAL
Otterspool Park
Liverpool L17 5AL
www.hubfestival.co.uk
Liverpool is home to some of the world's best skaters and breakers, and the UK's foremost free urban culture festival. Some twenty-odd thousand people turn up in May to catch BMX, inline skate and skateboarding demonstrations, breakdancing competitions, live music and much more.

The Hub Festival

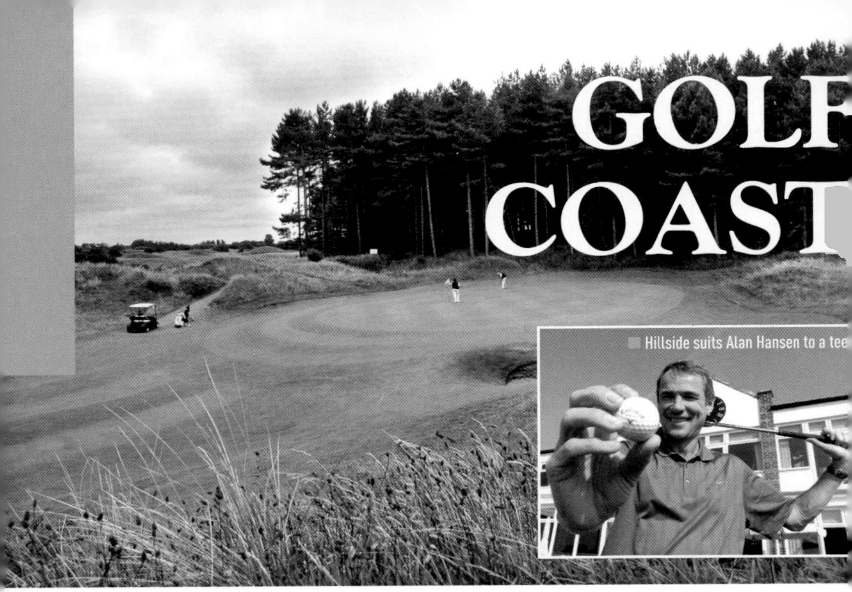

GOLF COAST

Hillside suits Alan Hansen to a tee

THE golf clubs created from this wild land have an international reputation.

Royal Birkdale and Southport, and Ainsdale, have hosted the Ryder Cup.

Birkdale is also a regular on The Open venue circuit, while West Lancashire, Formby, Hillside and Hesketh have staged major championships, amateur and professional representative matches for many years.

The Open Championship returns to Royal Liverpool in 2014 – just eight years after Tiger Woods won the claret jug. It will be the twelfth time the Hoylake links has hosted golf's oldest major.

Wirral's Royal Liverpool has also been announced as the venue for the prestigious 2012 Ricoh British Women's Open, the first time the club has hosted the competition. The inaugural Wirral Golf Classic, to be held in September 2010, is expected to attract 300 participants in its first year – and hopes to become a self-sustaining event by 2012. "England's Golf Coast" might sound like an extravagant claim, but one that few will argue about given the standard of golf on offer.

Top BBC commentator and soccer legend Alan Hansen has trodden many o the world's finest fairways – including Augusta National, home of The Masters but he always looks forward to playing a Hillside, the venue for his annual Golf Classic charity event in aid of The Roy Castle Lung Cancer Foundation.

"I can't think of a better course than Hillside," says Hansen, the former Liverpool and Scotland defender and a 2-handicapper.

"I might be biased, being a member there, but it really is a fantastic layout, easily one of the best in the country, and its back nine is second to none.

"Hillside is only one of many great courses in this area. You've got Hillside,

LISTINGS

FORMBY GOLF CLUB
Golf Road
Formby L37 1YH
01704 872 164
www.formbygolfclub.co.uk

One of the classic courses of the Lancashire coastline and has hosted many important events, particularly three Amateur Championships.

HESKETH
Cockle Dick's Lane
Southport PR9 9QQ
01704 536 897
www.heskethgolfclub.co.uk

The oldest golf club in Southport, established in 1885. Part links and part parkland, professional championship golf has been played at Hesketh from the early days. It is regularly chosen as a qualifying venue when The Open is played at nearby Royal Birkdale.

HILLSIDE
Hasting Road
Hillside PR8 2LU
01704 567 169
www.hillside-golfclub.co.uk

Hillside is widely regarded as the finest British golf course not to have staged an Open Championship, and there are those who believe that it presents a tougher challenge than many of the courses on the current rota.

ROYAL BIRKDALE
Waterloo Road
Birkdale PR8 2LX
01704 567 920
www.royalbirkdale.com

One of England's most illustrious courses having staged The Open in 1954, 1961, 1965, 1971, 1983, 1991, 1998 and 2008, The Amateur in 1946 and 1989, the Walker Cup in 1951 and the Ryder Cup in 1965 and 1969.

ROYAL LIVERPOOL
Meols Drive
Hoylake
Wirral CH47 4AL
0151 632 3101
www.royal-liverpool-golf.com

Built in 1869 and, with the exception of Westward Ho! in Devon, the oldest seaside course in England.

SOUTHPORT AND AINSDALE
Bradshaw's Lane
Ainsdale PR8 3LG
01704 578 000
www.sandagolfclub.co.uk

Better known locally as S&A, designed by five-time Open champion, James Braid.

WEST LANCS GOLF CLUB
Hall Road West
Blundellsands L23 8SZ
0151 924 1076
www.westlancashiregolf.co.uk

A pioneer of golf in the North West and among the top ten oldest clubs in England.

then Royal Birkdale right next door and then Southport and Ainsdale, all in a row along the same stretch of coastline.

"I can't think of anywhere else in the world where you can find three truly great courses literally neighbouring each other."

"Visitors to the area won't have a problem having a truly great time – there really are so many great courses on offer. But a lot of people come here and only think of playing Royal Birkdale and there are many more courses that are virtually unheard of that are almost, or just as good. Ormskirk, for example, is a great track and Hesketh is another one you shouldn't miss – it's an Open qualifying course and has some great holes.

"Formby is another world-class course, which offers some great views over the Irish Sea and is always in top condition.

"Then, further on, is West Lancs and Royal Liverpool. I also love Royal Lytham. For me that's right up there with Hillside and Birkdale. There really is something for everybody."

For more information visit www.englandsgolfcoast.com

Making waves

IT has seen some action in its time, the River Mersey.

Slave ships, famine boats, liners from all over the world, war-time vessels and, of course, the famous ferries across the Mersey – they have all relied on the river over the centuries. It may well be a little less busy these days, but it's still one of the best ways to see the city.

SAIL YOUR OWN BOAT

Liverpool Marina at Coburg Wharf offers sailors from all over England the chance to use their lock and has 400 berths available for use – and it's also home to Liverpool Yacht Club and the Merseyside Master Mariners.

HIRE A SHIP

For a more glamorous and upmarket time, why not get in touch with the folks at Mersey Ferries and hire a boat? Every ferry is equipped with its own cafe bar and promenade decks, and the scenery is breathtaking.

The famous Ferry Cross the Mersey is also available for hire these days too – with the flagship Royal Daffodil on the water again after a multi-million pound refurbishment.

THE VENICE OF MERSEYSIDE

The completion of a £22m restoration project has extended the Leeds-Liverpool canal, opening up the new Liverpool canal link to a new generation of sailors.

By extending the canal through the disused central docks, across the Pier Head in front of the Three Graces and into the south docks, the restoration project has created a further 1.4 miles of navigable waterway. It's official – canal hopping is cool again.

TAKE THE SPORTING OPTION

Canoes are also popular in and around the docks by the Mersey – Liverpool Canoe Club comes highly recommended, and they welcome beginners and more experienced people alike. Other water sports such as swimming, water skiing and polo are all active by the river and Liverpool City Council offers an excellent range of days out, courses and fun-filled learner sessions for you to enjoy.

FITNESS

British Military Fitness in Sefton Park

ARK HEALTH & FITNESS
Radisson Hotel
109 Old Hall Street
Liverpool L3 9BD
0151 966 1999
www.arkspafitness.com

DAVID LLOYD
5 The Aerodrome
Speke L24 8QD
0151 494 4000
www.davidlloyd.co.uk

THE GYM LIVERPOOL
One Park West
Liverpool L1 8LT
0844 412 8135
www.thegymgroup.com

GREENS HEALTH & FITNESS
1 Riverside Drive
Liverpool L3 4EN
0151 707 6000
www.greensfitness.co.uk

THE HARBOUR CLUB
Crowne Plaza Liverpool
Princes Dock, Pier Head
Liverpool L3 1QW
0151 243 8000
www.cpliverpool.com

LA FITNESS
88 Rose Lane
Mossley Hill
Liverpool L18 8AG
0843 170 1074
www.lafitness.co.uk

LIFESTYLES MILLENNIUM
Millennium House
Victoria Street
Liverpool L1 6DL
0151 233 4123
www.liverpool.gov.uk

LIVERPOLE POLE DANCE ACADEMY
www.liverpole.co.uk
A fun way to banish those bingo wings and improve your body's core, Liverpole's fitness pole dance classes are taught by experienced instructors with sport, fitness or dance backgrounds. Liverpole's women-only courses are carefully structured, featuring a warm-up pole dance routine, a section focused on body conditioning and cool down. Courses are available in Bootle and Fazakerley.

BRITISH MILITARY FITNESS
www.britmilfit.com
If you fancy being put through your paces by former members of the armed forces with recognised fitness qualifications, give these classes in Calderstones Park and Sefton Park a try. Ideal for anyone who wants to get fit in a fun, social and motivated environment, the classes are suitable for all abilities.

SYNERGY FITNESS CAMPS
www.synergyfitnesscamps.com
Synergy combine stretching and intense body conditioning to create individual workout sessions that get great results through the latest proven training techniques and nutrition advice.

SHOPPING

Late-night shopping at Liverpool ONE

HOW can you tell that you're shopping in Liverpool?

The streets are packed, there's a lavish helping of style and fashion stores, and somewhere a lone guitarist is playing Can't Buy Me Love.

Outside Liverpool ONE - and it's almost big enough to qualify as a separate city - the Albert Dock has some fabulous art and craft shops, as well as souvenirs galore.

But the main drag is Church Street with Cavern Walks and Bold Street at either end. All the big department and chain stores are present, including Next, River Island, Marks & Spencer, Top Shop, Primark and Schuh, but it's the unique boutiques and independents that will really float your boat, becoming more quirky the further you venture up Bold Street and along super-eclectic Renshaw Street.

With the Metquarter offering the likes of Diesel, Hugo Boss, Levi's, Firetrap and Peter Werth, shoppers really are spoilt for choice. How will your credit card cope?

HARDMAN STREET

BULLET
41 Hardman Street
Liverpool L1 9AS
0151 708 5808
Vintage or new? It's a perennial fashion dilemma – but Bullet has the best of both worlds. Joanne Denton sells her own designs in vintage fabrics alongside originals from the 60s, 70s and 80s. And it's that uniqueness which has a big appeal.

BOLD STREET

HOPE & WINKLE VINTAGE
Petticoat Lane Arcade
Liverpool L1 4HY
Helen Hope has brought new meaning to the old adage 'all that glitters is not gold' with an exciting new range of bespoke jewellery made entirely from reclaimed items.

LIVERPOOL WORLD SHOP
71 Bold Street
Liverpool L1 4EZ
A not-for-profit organisation specialising in selling fair trade products. Browse amongst floaty fabrics, exotic textiles and hand crafted knick knacks that you never knew you needed.

NEWS FROM NOWHERE
96 Bold Street
Liverpool L1 4HY
0151 708 7270
Liverpool's radical & community bookshop sells books, t-shirts and more.

The Resurrection team

PROBE RECORDS
9 Slater Street
Liverpool L1 4BW
0151 708 8815
Original, and still the best, glam queen Pete Burns' old vinyl emporium is now just off Bold Street. Specialising in reissue vinyl, you'll find independent sounds, classic 60s, 70s, psych, garage, punk, dubstep and much more.

RESURRECTION
17-19 Bold Street
Liverpool L1 4DN
0151 709 2676
Our favourite indie clothes store is slowly taking over Bold Street. Girls can pop downstairs to Resurrection's vintage section to raid the drawers for one of a kind accessories and dresses. Lads aren't left out either, as the men's vintage section boasts gentlemen's scarves and classic trilby hats.

SIZE?
59 Bold Street
Liverpool L1 4EZ
0151 707 8813
If you've got a Converse fetish or simply like to rock a nice pair of Adidas Originals, this place is a must for all sneaker heads.

UTILITY
60/86 Bold Street
Liverpool L1 4EA
0151 708 4192
Find the city's very best range of contemporary furniture, lighting and home accessories in the larger store. Further along Bold Street is the Gift Store where you'll find a gorgeous, inspirational range of cool greetings cards, jewellery, watches and great items for giving and treating yourself!

Dick Mawdsley,owner of Utility on Bold Street

RENSHAW STREET

GRAND CENTRAL HALL
Renshaw Street
Liverpool L1 2SF
Liverpool's alternative scene might have lost Quiggins under Liverpool ONE, but it did gain the amazing Grand Central. With 50 retailers all under one roof, the Grade II listed Grand Central Hall offers an eclectic mix of shops from vintage clothes and fine arts to underwear, shoes, hairdressing, tattoos – everything the discerning shopper could possibly need!

RAIDER'S VINTAGE
38 Renshaw Street
Liverpool L1 4EF
0151 709 2929
There's always a fantastic selection of vintage accessories and dresses on offer at this treasure trove of a dressing up box.

CAVERN WALKS

BOUDOIR BOUTIQUE
1 Cavern Walks
0151 236 6001
This elegant boutique is every girl's dream with its beautiful vintage lamps and chaise longue, not to mention the lovely designer frocks on display. Big fans of the boutique include Corrie's Michelle Keegan, Hollyoaks' Carley Stenson and Ricky Whittle's Strictly Come Dancing partner, Natalie Lowe, has also been papped perusing at some sequined little numbers.

Cavern Walks

CRICKET
10 Cavern Walks
0151 227 4645
Everyone who's anyone shops here. A beautifully-laid out boutique, it stocks all those Missoni, Stella McCartney, Pucci, Juicy Couture and Chloe must-haves you've been promising yourself.

CHRISTOPHER JAMES JEWELLERS
7 Cavern Walks
0151 236 0460
This trendsetting store sells unique pieces of jewellery created using handcrafted gemstones from all over the world. Plus a bespoke custom made engagement and wedding ring service.

LOLA LOVES
5 Cavern Walks
0151 236 6163
Liverpool is falling in love with Lola. Local designer Debbie Bogg's catwalk-inspired bespoke designs mean it's already proving a magnet for the glitterati.

VIVIENNE WESTWOOD
Cavern Walks
0151 227 2700
One of the group's flagship boutiques housing the full range of collections from the Grande Dame of British Fashion. Gold Label, Red Label, Anglomania and MAN menswear sit beautifully alongside a comprehensive selection of accessories, jewellery and small leather goods.

METQUARTER

ALL-SAINTS
Metquarter
0151 227 9804
A range of stylish clothing for the youth of the city.

DIESEL
Metquarter
0151 227 3729
When Renzo Rosso founded Diesel, he wanted to be a fashion leader, an innovator, and a pioneer. There's little in today's fashion market that rivals Diesel's original designs and production.

FIRETRAP
Metquarter
0151 227 2857
Caution: Use only with a thirst for chic. Firetrap's quirky range of stylish clothing for men and women will appeal to anyone.

FLANNELS
Metquarter
0151 236 0552
Designer products and understated elegance in fashion have made Flannels a prestigious and well established retailer.

The Metquarter

FOSSIL
Metquarter
0151 242 0070
Looking for the perfect belt or handbag to compliment your newly acquired attire? The Metquarter branch of Fossil offers an extensive line of men's and women's fashion accessories ranging from watches and jewellery to sunglasses and apparel.

KATE KUBA
Metquarter
0151 227 4777
Shoes, shoes, shoes . . . a girl just can't get enough. The ethos for this women's designer shoe shop isn't just to sell beautiful shoes – Kate Kuba sells exquisite style.

MAC COSMETICS
Metquarter
0870 192 5050
Founded to support the creative needs of professional make-up artists, MAC stands at the epicentre of fashion, beauty and popular culture.

TOMMY HILFIGER
Metquarter
0151 227 1354
One of the most recognisable fashion names in the world can be found in the Metquarter and boasts a wide selection of men's and women's urban clothing as well as the famous fragrances.

The Metquarter

WHITECHAPEL

POP BOUTIQUE
58 Whitechapel
Liverpool L1 6EG
0151 709 7858
Featuring its own Pop label and vintage on the ground floor, while upstairs you'll find lots of ladies wear dating back to the Fifties, as well as cool retro junk.

A-Z OF LIVERPOOL ONE

EMMA JOHNSON's A-Z guide to Europe's biggest retail and leisure development

A is for American Apparel

Liverpool ONE is home to the UK's first American Apparel store outside London.

B is for Beauty

Inside the flagship Debenhams store you will find brands such as Urban Decay, Clinique, Yves Saint Laurent and Estee Lauder. John Lewis's store is home to exclusive beauty brands like Sisley, Decleor, Prescriptives, Dr Hauscka and La Prairie.

C is for Chavasse Park

Providing an outdoor landscaped area between the shopping complex and the Strand, Chavasse Park is a stunning five acres of green space surrounded by trees.

D is for Designers

Label junkies can get their fix at the likes of Ted Baker, Jigsaw, Karen Millen, Urban Outfitters, Pull & Bear, Mango, Fred Perry, Hollister, Jaeger, Lacoste and G Star.

E is for Europe's biggest

With more than 160 shops and restaurants, two new hotels, a 14-screen cinema, a five-acre park, residential and office accommodation, Liverpool ONE is the largest urban regeneration project in Europe.

G is for GAP

Take a trip to the Gap if you're looking for casual style for men, women or well-dressed babies.

H is for Habitat

The first Habitat store in the city for 20 years is 20,000 sq ft and spread over two floors.

I is for iPod

Whether you are looking to upgrade or purchase your first, then you will find everything at Liverpool's first Apple store.

J is for Jewellery

Pandora and Swarovski enthuse fashionistas and classic jewellery lovers alike.

F is for Food

Restaurants at Liverpool ONE include Barburitto, Pret a Manger, Dinomat, Zizzi, Nandos, Wagamama, Gourmet Burger Kitchen, Red Hot Buffet and Yo! Sushi!

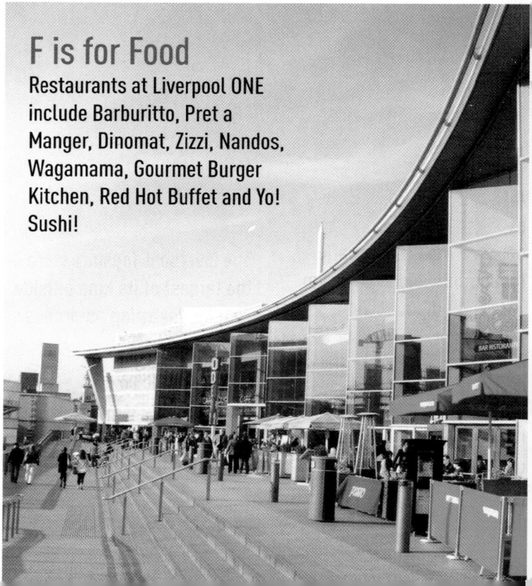

K is for Keys Court

Formerly home to HMV, this stunning frontage on Church Street provides a grand entrance to the development.

L is for League of Their Own

Liverpool ONE is home to the new LFC store, the biggest official club store in Europe, and the cleverly named Everton Two, Liverpool ONE.

M is for Movies

Cinema fans can enjoy all the latest blockbusters at the amazing 14-screen Odeon multiplex.

N is for Nike

Whether it is trainers you want or sportswear, you are sure to find something you fancy in the sports giant's first Liverpool store.

O is for One Park West

A 17-storey building designed by Cesar Pelli and comprising apartments, offices, parking, restaurants and even a gym. Just don't distract them on the treadmill.

P is for Pukka

Celebrity chef Jamie Oliver opens his 11th 'Jamie's Italian' at Paradise Place in June 2010.

Q is for Q Park

With over 3,000 parking spaces you should find somewhere to leave the car.

R is for Republic

One of the UK's leading sellers of premium branded clothing including G Star, Bench and Henleys.

S is for Student discount

Impoverished students have no need to dress scruffily any more. All Saints, Office, and Bank are among the stores offering money off for those in higher education.

T is for Topshop

The Liverpool Topshop store is the largest of its kind outside London, featuring numerous must-have brands.

U is for Underwear

Whether it's lingerie from the La Senza store, Leia or Ann Summers, women are well supported in Liverpool ONE.

V is for Views

From Debenhams, One Park West and the Hilton Hotel, the views of the city are magnificent.

W is for Wall Street

One of the new streets, named in recognition of the walls of the old Liverpool Castle and to mark the historic trading links between Liverpool and the US.

X is for eX-tended opening hours

(OK, we cheated a little bit there). With stores open until 8pm, Monday to Friday, and until 7pm on Saturday, you will always be able to find time to shop.

Y is for Yee Rah

One of the newest dining experiences to land at Liverpool ONE, and from the same restaurant stable that brought us the uber-glamorous Chaopraya.

Z is for Zzzzzz . . .

After all that shopping, you're bound to be exhausted. The Hilton, Novotel and Bridge Street serviced apartments are all just a stone's throw from Liverpool ONE.

Andrew & Liz Collinge in the Castle Street salon

HEALTH & BEAUTY

GIVEN any chance to get glammed up, the ladies – and gents – of Liverpool will be filling the salons, spas and boutiques around the city and beyond.

You can't claim style status with rollers in your hair and still be in your PJs now, can you . . . well actually it seems you can!

Within the city centre there's a beauty box full to choose from, including Barbara Daley; highly acclaimed in Liverpool and synonymous with quality, this salon has been working its magic on clients for 20 years. Andrew Collinge is another fine example of creativity and expertise in the city. Starting his hairdressing career in Liverpool in 1974 Andrew opened his first salon 25 years ago in Wirral, and so the journey began. Spending eight years on 'This Morning' completing makeovers, then offering a service at Harrods, TV shows, not to mention the launch of hair care products and appliances. Experience the experts at Andrew Collinge Hair and Beauty salon on Castle Street which offers hair care to luxury massage, reflexology and make-up to go.

Herbert has become a proud, key Liverpool figure in the hair and beauty industry, serving Merseyside for 45 years.

His knowledge and experience shine through the team at Herbert of Liverpool on Hanover Street, with his young fashion stylists joined by outstanding artistic directors. Unisex salon Hooka has built up an impressive celeb client list, and managing director Dion Padan was named a cut above the rest at the Nation's Favourite Hairdresser Awards 2009.

Dion's salon on Wood Street branched out into women's beauty, but specialises in male facials, tanning and waxing and is always busy.

LISTINGS

ANDREW COLLINGE
Castle Chambers
41-45 Castle Street
Liverpool L2 9TJ
0151 227 2366
www.andrewcollinge.com

ARK SPA
Radisson Blu
109 Old Hall Street
Liverpool L3 9BD
0151 966 1999
www.arkspafitness.com

BARBARA DALEY
29-31 Lime Street Liverpool
L1 1JG
0151 709 7974
www.barbaradaleyhair.co.uk

BODY CONSCIOUS
206 Aigburth Road
Liverpool L17 9PE
0151 727 7400
www.bodyconsciousliverpool.com

CHILL OUT SPA
Stanley Grange
Ormskirk Road
Knowsley Park L34 4AR
0844 9670 599
www.chilloutspa.co.uk

HERBERT OF LIVERPOOL
69 Hanover Street
Liverpool L1 3DY
0151 709 7834
www.herbertofliverpool.co.uk

HOOKA
92/98 Wood Street
Liverpool L1 4DQ
0151 708 0302
www.hooka-uk.com

LASH OUT LASH BAR
MetQuarter
Liverpool L1 6DA
0151 531 1177
www.lashoutlashesuk.com

LITTLE DAY SPA
Oxford Road
Brighton-Le-Sands
Liverpool L22 7RW
0151 928 1029
www.littledayspaltd.co.uk

ORIGIN REJUVENATION CLINIC
16 Castle Street
Liverpool
0151 236 6086
www.originrejuvenationclinic.co.uk

SCIN
4 Keys Court
Liverpool ONE
0151 709 8710
www.scin.uk.com

VOODOU
98 Bold Street
Liverpool L1 4HY
0844 445 7889
www.voodou.co.uk

For style and beauty treatments try the recently opened Scin in Liverpool ONE or Lash Out Lashes in Metquarter or maybe the award-winning Voodou hair and beauty which has grown to six salons and barbers around the city.

For a complete pamper session there are numerous luxurious spa facilities around Merseyside where you can relax and unwind. In the city centre is Ark Spa at the Radisson Blu on Old Hall Street, or Origin Rejuvenation on Castle Street where you can have an ultimate luxury day spa package. Outside the city one of the most exclusive spas in Merseyside is Chill Out Spa within the stunning grounds of Knowsley Hall. The spa is famed for its sumptuous facilities including a wonderful lagoon spa, chill-out pods, Turkish steam showers, wide range of face and body therapies as well as nail and beauty treatments.

Emma Thompson

Pools of seawater shimmer on Formby Beach

FROM the bracing parade of Parkgate, to the Gormley iron men in Crosby and the red squirrels and pinewoods of Formby, this truly is a region surrounded by the great outdoors.

Speke and Garston Coastal Reserve is a breath of fresh air – once the site of the old Liverpool Airport, the reserve features meadows and wildlife habitats, interwoven with footpaths and cycle trails, and you can spot wading birds.

Another of the region's hidden gems is the delightful, unspoiled Hale Village.

Home to the grave of the famous Child of Hale, and Hale Lighthouse, the village also offers a route to one of the best walks along the river Mersey and another great day out.

The best views of Liverpool are from Wirral – New Brighton's promenade is a good place to start, and from here you can capture a picture-postcard of a majestic skyline on a par with Manhattan or Shanghai.

Leasowe Lighthouse, Britain's oldest brick-built lighthouse dating from 1763, stands 27 metres tall on the North Wirral foreshore, with views of Bidston, Caldy, the Welsh hills and out over the Irish Sea.

The lighthouse houses a Visitor Centre and is the base for the Coastal Rangers and the focal point for the North Wirral Coastal Park.

For more than 70 years from the height of the Victorian era to the early 1960s a busy railway ran from Hooton, near Chester to West Kirby. Now this 12-mile Wirral Way forms the backbone of the splendid Wirral Country Park, the first designated country park in Britain. Seven miles of the route run alongside the Dee Estuary, a haven for seabirds.

A good place to start an outing is the country park visitor centre at Thurstaston, if for no other reason than to pick up a leaflet highlighting the delights of this park of contrasts. From the sheltered inland quiet of the Wirral Way where badgers and foxes hunt in the shadows to the 60-ft cliffs overlooking the Dee where you can enjoy the sights, sounds and smells of the sea, this park is a true oasis of peace.

When the tide is out, the walk across the mud flats from West Kirby to Hilbre Island is quite breathtaking – it must be stressed that this walk must be taken with great care after checking tide times. On the horizon are the snow-peaked mountain tops of Wales. The walk takes just under an hour, and it's worth taking a picnic and seal spotting once you're there.

It is sometimes called the port that the sea forgot, but Parkgate has been charming visitors for centuries and still does. The composer Handel is believed to have put the finishing touches to his Messiah here, before sailing to Dublin for its premiere.

In Sefton, from the end of the docks at Seaforth to Southport there are 22 miles of coast. Formby Point is the fourth largest dune system in the country. At the National Trust site at Freshfield you can enjoy a stroll through the pinewoods – on the lookout for those elusive red squirrels – and enjoy a stunning stretch of unspoilt coastline and beautiful dunes, home to an array of rare wildlife such as the natterjack toad and northern dune tiger beetles.

Antony Gormley's Another Place at Crosby Beach is an incredible sight – the iron men, sculpted on Gormley's own body, are both strange and beautiful, as they stare out towards the horizon. Unmissable.

Tony Martin

Wild at heart

MERSEYSIDE is an amazing place for wildlife – from badgers to grey seals, it has got the lot.

There are so many places that are perfect for families to start enjoying the natural world – Parkgate Marshes on a high tide for birds, Red Rocks for more birds, dragonflies and flora, Hilbre for a priceless island experience, the Wirral Way for birds, insects and plants. In Formby, Cabin Hill, south of Range Lane, the dunes and pinewoods, Wicks Lane pond, Fisherman's Path and, of course, the National Trust Reserve at Victoria Road, Freshfield, for our threatened red squirrels.

The Crosby Marine Park and the footpath towards Hightown north of Hall Road and the Coastguard Station in Litherland, the Rimrose Valley is wonderful.

Birding and the natural world can be enjoyed at all levels and it's free. How can you put a price on an Arctic tern or Manx shearwater skimming past Formby Point in a storm? Or a dragonfly glittering over a summer pond?

Every day is a thrill, but, if I had to choose just one thing, it would have to be watching Leach's petrels as they are blown into Liverpool Bay on autumn gales.

Magnificent!

John Dempsey

Reception at the Hilton Hotel

LISTINGS

HIGH END

62 CASTLE STREET
Castle Street
Liverpool L2 7LQ
0151 702 7898
www.62castlest.com

A stunning, modern and exclusive city centre boutique hotel, formerly known as the Trials Hotel. Using a contemporary interior with a traditional twist, the design contradicts but complements the beautiful Victorian architecture. This hotel is in a fantastic location, just moments away from both the business district and Liverpool's cosmopolitan nightlife.

ATLANTIC TOWER THISTLE
Chapel Street
Liverpool L3 9RE
0845 305 8325
www.thistle.com

The Thistle Liverpool is situated in a prime location for the city centre, close to the Pier Head, business district and Liverpool ONE. The hotel has 225 bedrooms, some boasting magnificent views over the city's greatest landmarks. Guests will appreciate the excellent air conditioned accommodation, choice of bars and restaurants and the friendly and attentive service.

CROWNE PLAZA
St Nicholas Place
Princes Dock
Liverpool L3 1QW
0151 243 8000

Located near the Pier Head and overlooking the River Mersey, the Crowne Plaza Hotel in Liverpool city centre provides guests with outstanding standards of comfort and service. Excellent facilities and first class customer service ensure your stay is a pleasant one. To get the most out of your stay, you can take advantage of the health club – the Harbour Club – or sample a delicious range of modern and international dishes in the contemporary surroundings of the Plaza Brasserie.

HARD DAYS NIGHT HOTEL

Central Buildings
North John Street
Liverpool L2 6RR
0151 236 1964
www.harddaysnighthotel.com

If your raison d'etre is to come to Liverpool and you're coming because of the Fab Four, then the £20m Beatles-inspired boutique hotel is your ideal base.
The hotel was officially launched in 2008 with a glitzy opening party attended by John Lennon's half-sister Julia Baird. In the heart of the Cavern Quarter, the hotel is elegantly furnished, each room including state-of-the-art technical facilities.

The Lennon Suite at the Hard Days Night Hotel

HILTON HOTEL

3 Thomas Steers Way
Liverpool L1 8LW
0151 708 4200
www.hilton.co.uk

Opened in 2009, this £55m hotel is a landmark property with spectacular views over the Liver Buildings, Albert Dock and Chavasse Park. The 215-room hotel reputedly has the most expensive room in the city – its luxurious Presidential Suite, which has views across the waterfront. Keep fit while you travel in the Fitness Centre, watch the world go by as you savour delicious cuisine in the Exchange Restaurant, which overlooks Chavasse Park, or relax with a drink in the contemporary Pima bar.

HOPE STREET HOTEL

40 Hope Street
Liverpool L1 9DA
0151 709 3000

Liverpool's award-winning boutique hotel, sitting pretty between two magnificent cathedrals. 89 individually designed hotel rooms, solid wood floors warmed by under floor heating and king sized

Hope Street Hotel

beds draped in Egyptian cotton. Wall mounted LCD wide screen TVs, DVD and CD players and Arne Jacobsen telephones, along with complimentary broadband access in every room. Built in 1860 in the style of a Venetian palazzo, Hope Street is a delightful, privately-owned, design hotel, passionately run with thoughtful service and comfortable contemporary interiors.

MALMAISON LIVERPOOL

William Jessop Way
Princes Dock
Liverpool L3 1QZ
0151 229 5000
www.malmaison-liverpool.com

The sleek architecture of this hotel, the 10th Malmaison in the family, blends with the modern design and sophisticated facilities within. This dazzling boutique hotel in Liverpool offers breathtaking Manhattan style with a special twist of Mal. The brasserie serves simple, tasty cuisine and the Plum Bar, with its fine wines and signature cocktails, has become a Liverpool hot spot. Other Malmaison facilities include a state-of-the-art gym and function rooms.

MARRIOTT LIVERPOOL
1 Queen Square
Liverpool L1 1RH
0151 476 8000
www.marriott.co.uk

Set within the art and cultural district, overlooking Queen Square and within walking distance to Lime Street train station, the World Museum and Empire theatre. After a day of museum hopping or shopping, enjoy a swim in the indoor pool or a relaxing dinner at Olivier's.

NOVOTEL LIVERPOOL
40 Hanover Street
Liverpool L1 4LN
0151 702 5100
www.novotel.com

The Novotel brand arrived in Liverpool in 2009 with the opening of a 209-room four-star hotel, on the city's Hanover Street. The 12-storey contemporary building, styled by Belgian interior designer Patrick Dumont, includes a new self check-in and check-out service, in-room entertainment systems and high-speed internet access.

Novotel Liverpool

The onsite fitness suite, steam room and relaxation pool are perfect for making your stay invigorating or relaxing. The Elements Restaurant and Bar offers 24 hour wide ranging cuisine and there is an onsite fitness suite, steam room and relaxation pool. A great central location near all of the city's shopping, nightlife and cultural hot-spots.

PARR STREET HOTEL
33-45 Parr Street
Liverpool L1 4JN
0151 707 1050
www.parrstreet.co.uk

Parr Street Hotel is housed within the famous Parr Street Studios, near the Ropewalks area of the city with its buzzing nightlife. Designed by Gary Millar, all 12 rooms are boho chic, funky, warm and modern with leather sleigh beds, NASA inspired memory mattresses, power showers, the latest fat boy beanbag, LCD TV's with digital channels and mini bar.

RADISSON BLU LIVERPOOL
107 Old Hall Street
Liverpool L3 9BD
0151 966 1500
www.radissonblu.co.uk

Located on the city's breathtaking waterfront, the stylish and ubercool Radisson Blu is situated in the heart of Liverpool's business district with breathtaking views over the river Mersey and an interior with its own style and artistic flair. 194 stylishly designed bedrooms, the exclusive River Suite with its own lounge, dining room, en-suite bedroom and kitchen, Filini an exquisite 1 AA rosette Italian themed restaurant, The White Bar offering a perfect place to relax and enjoy creative cocktails and Ark Health & Fitness, the hotel's mini sanctuary.

The Sir Thomas Hotel

SIR THOMAS HOTEL
24 Sir Thomas Street
Liverpool L1 6JB
0151 236 1366
www.sirthomashotel.co.uk

This boutique hotel offers the discerning guest exceptional quality in accommodation, food and service. The hotel is situated in the heart of Liverpool city centre, near the Cavern Quarter and business district. Situated in the old Bank of Liverpool building, the hotel offers a delicate blend of Liverpool's history and modern culture. The restaurant and bar is everything you would expect from dining in a top hotel, full of classic British style and sophistication, with an added contemporary twist.

APARTMENTS

BRIDGESTREET AT LIVERPOOL ONE
39 Paradise Street
Liverpool L1 3ED
020 7792 2222
www.bridgestreet.co.uk

These centrally located apartments offer a choice of stylish one, two and three-bedroom apartments. All of the apartments are fitted out to the highest specification throughout and have contemporary, fully functional kitchens and beautiful bathrooms. Situated at the centre of everything, just a short walk from Liverpool ONE, Concert Square and the Cavern Quarter, with impressive views over the city. Apartments are available on a daily, weekly, or monthly basis.

Staybridge Suites

PREMIER APARTMENTS EDEN SQUARE
7 Hatton Garden
Liverpool L3 2FE
0151 227 9467
www.premierapartmentsliverpool.com

These apartments offer a mixture of one and two bedroom accommodation. There are 63 guest rooms over seven floors, all accessible by a lift. Each has a fully furnished bedroom, bathroom, sitting room, dining area and kitchen. Located in the business district, about 10 minutes walk to the Albert Dock.

SIGNATURE LIVING SERVICED APARTMENTS
38-40 Victoria Street
Liverpool L1 6BX
0151 236 0166
www.signatureliving.co.uk

City centre location in the heart of Liverpool's vibrant bars, clubs and restaurants. 12 apartments, including four duplux apartments, sleeping up to 15 people.

STAYBRIDGE SUITES
21 Keel Wharf
Liverpool L3 4FN
0871 423 4931
www.staybridge.co.uk

An all-suite, extended-stay hotel that caters to guests looking for just one night, one week or longer. Staybridge Suites offer two types of suites: studio and one-bedroom. All have a kitchen, living room area, work space, flat screen TV and free Wi-Fi.

Signature Living Apartments

MID-PRICE HOTELS

THE BRITANNIA ADELPHI HOTEL
Ranelagh Place
Liverpool L3 5UL
0871 222 0029
www.britanniahotels.com

The Adelphi Hotel first opened its doors (if, technically, you can open revolving doors) in 1826, and, over a century-and-three-quarters later it's still our most famous – if no longer our grandest – hotel. This is where it all started, with Roy Rogers and Trigger proving to be the hotel's most famous guests. In 1954 Roy Rogers and his wife were in the hotel ill with flu, while horse Trigger wandered around the reception and famously walked up the staircase and made his way to the hotel room. Other distinguished guests, and possibly better behaved, have included famous authors Charles Dickens and Mark Twain. Today, reviews of the hotel are very mixed, but the Edwardian style still turns heads.

THE DOLBY HOTEL
Queen's Dock
Liverpool L3 4DE
0151 708 7272
www.dolbyhotels.co.uk

Ideally situated on the dock road near Liverpool ONE, The Dolby offers good value for money and a friendly service.

EXPRESS BY HOLIDAY INN
Britannia Pavilion
Albert Dock
Liverpool L3 4AD
08448 757575
www.hiexpress.com

A group of 19th century Grade I listed warehouses, made entirely from cast iron and red brick, beautifully renovated and offering 135 bedrooms. The Lively Express Bar has picturesque views of the inner dock. Great location for central attractions.

THE FEATHERS HOTEL
115-125 Mount Pleasant
Liverpool L3 5TF
0151 709 9655
www.feathers.uk.com

Situated near Liverpool University and Hope Street, The Feathers offers standard rooms to luxury suites, all at excellent value for money prices, including the famous 'Eat As Much As You Like' breakfast.

IBIS LIVERPOOL
27 Wapping
Liverpool L1 8LY
0151 706 9800
www.ibishotel.com

Offers 127 rooms including five for guests with limited mobility, a restaurant, a bar offering snacks 24hrs and pay secure outdoor parking. Business guests will appreciate use of WiFi Internet.

JURY'S INN
Keel Wharf
Liverpool L3 4FN
0151 244 3777
liverpoolhotels.jurysinns.com

A popular 3-star hotel located at Kings Waterfront, adjacent to the Albert Dock and directly opposite the BT Convention Centre and Echo Arena, close to all the main business and shopping areas. Spacious and comfortable rooms are all en-suite and can accommodate three adults, two adults and two children, or just one person in complete comfort.

THE LINER AT LIVERPOOL
Lord Nelson Street
Liverpool L3 5QB
0151 709 7050
www.sterlinghotels.com

Formerly The Gladstone, the nautical themed Liner promises to transport guests back to the golden age of ocean travel, when only the highest standards of comfort, quality and service would suffice. From the brass portholes to the welcoming and dedicated crew, The Liner bears all the authentic hallmarks of the world's finest cruise ships.

PREMIER INN LIVERPOOL ALBERT DOCK
East Britannia Building
Albert Dock
Liverpool L3 4AD
0870 990 6432
www.premierinn.com

In the heart of Liverpool Albert Dock, this Premier Inn makes an ideal base to explore the local surrounds. With local attractions including the Liverpool ECHO Arena, Liverpool ONE shopping centre, Tate Art Gallery and the Beatles Story, this is a very popular location.

PREMIER INN LIVERPOOL CITY CENTRE
Vernon Street
Liverpool L2 2AY
0870 2383323
www.premierinn.com

A great city centre location, conveniently located for all amenities and attractions. Close to Mathew Street, the Gay Quarter and St George's Hall.

BUDGET

AACHEN HOTEL
89-91 Mount Pleasant
Liverpool L3 5TB
0151 709 3477
www.aachenhotel.co.uk

Popular family-owned business housed within a Georgian Grade II building, offering fine accommodation, friendly service and great value. Close to Hope Street and the University of Liverpool. A variety of rooms are available, with and without en-suite facilities, including single, double, triple and quad rooms.

FORMULE ONE
25 Wapping
Liverpool L1 8LY
0151 709 2040
www.accorhotels.com

A cheap, no frills hotel in a good central location, perfect for nightlife.

THE NIGHTINGALE LODGE
1 Princes Road
Liverpool L8 1TG
www.thenightingalelodge.co.uk

This backpackers' lodge offers budget shared and private accommodation in the diverse Georgian Quarter of South Liverpool, only five minutes' walk from the city centre. There is no curfew, and reception is open 24 hours a day. The hostel has a welcoming atmosphere and a wealth of history. A good-value base for students to explore Liverpool.

YHA LIVERPOOL
25 Tabley Street
Liverpool L1 8EE
0845 371 9527
www.yha.org.uk

This Youth Hostel Assocation accommodation off Wapping, is a modern facility just ten minutes walk from the main attractions and nightlife. Bargain prices but clean, tidy and very friendly.

GETTING HERE

JOHN LENNON AIRPORT

Speke L24 1YD
0871 521 8484
www.liverpoolairport.com
JLA's airlines include two of Europe's largest low cost airlines, easyJet and Ryanair, as well as Wizz Air, Flybe and KLM. Destinations include Dublin, Paris, Amsterdam, Malaga, Belfast, Faro, Aberdeen, Barcelona, Alicante, Tenerife, Geneva, Riga, Palma De Mallorca, Oslo, Stockholm, Krakow and Berlin. The shuttle bus Airlink 501 travels from Liverpool John Lennon Airport to Liverpool South Parkway. To get to the city centre, you can take the Arriva Airlink 500 express (every 30 minutes) or local Arriva services 86A, 80A, 82A.

TERRAVISION COACH SERVICE

www.terravision.eu
From Liverpool JLA to Sackville Street, Manchester takes just 60 minutes. Coaches depart every hour from Liverpool John Lennon Airport outside the Arrivals Hall near the Yellow Submarine. Pre-book or pay on board.

NATIONAL EXPRESS COACHES

Norton Street
Liverpool L3 8LR
08717 818178
www.nationalexpress.com

LIME STREET STATION

Network Rail
Lime Street L1 1JD
National Rail
Enquiries 08457 48 49 50
Traintracker 0870 200 49 50
www.nationalrail.co.uk

NORFOLKLINE FERRIES

0844 499 0007
www.norfolkline.com
Operate ferries from Liverpool (Birkenhead) to Dublin and Belfast.

P&O IRISH SEA

Gladstone Dock
Liverpool Freeport
Liverpool L20 1PG
0871 66 44 777
www.poirishsea.com
Ferries from Liverpool to Dublin. The ferry terminal is about five miles from the city centre.

STEAM PACKET

Princes Parade
Liverpool L3 1DL
08722 992 992
www.steam-packet.com
Operating from a new terminal and car marshalling area at the Pier Head, the Steam Packets run between Liverpool and the Isle of Man.

TOURIST INFORMATION

THE 08 PLACE

Whitechapel
Liverpool L1 6DZ

ALBERT DOCK VISITOR INFORMATION CENTRE

Anchor Courtyard
Liverpool L3 4AF

LIVERPOOL JOHN LENNON AIRPORT TIC

Arrival Hall South Terminal
Speke Hall Avenue
Liverpool L24
Telephone Enquiries
0151 233 2008

ACCESS GUIDES

www.disabledgo.com

GETTING AROUND

MERSEYTRAVEL

www.merseytravel.gov.uk
Merseytravel Traveline:
Telephone 0871 200 22 33
Textphone users can dial 18001 then 0871 200 22 33 for a typetalk assisted call. When travelling by bus, you can either pay the driver when you board, or a variety of pre-paid bus tickets are available. Plusbus is a discount price ticket for unlimited bus travel that you buy with your train ticket. Saveaways are cheap, one-day tickets that you can use for travel on buses, trains and ferries in Merseyside during off-peak times. Season tickets include Solo for any bus at any time, and Trio for buses, trains and Mersey Ferries. When travelling on the Merseyrail network, you must pay the correct fare for your journey in advance at the station or face a £20 fine.

PARADISE STREET TRAVEL CENTRE

Paradise Street Interchange
1 Canning Place
Liverpool L1 8LB
9am – 5.30pm Mondays to Saturdays
10am – 4pm Sundays

QUEEN SQUARE TRAVEL CENTRE
Queen Square
Liverpool L1 1RG
9am – 5.30pm Mondays to Saturdays
10am – 5.30pm first Tuesday of every month
10.30am – 4.30pm Sundays

BIRKENHEAD TRAVEL CENTRE
Birkenhead Bus Station
Claughton Road
Birkenhead CH41 6RT
9.30am – 5pm Mondays to Saturdays

MERSEY FERRIES
www.merseyferries.co.uk

MERSEY TUNNELS
www.merseytunnels.co.uk

STAGECOACH UK BUS
www.stagecoachbus.com

TAXIS

HACKNEY CABS
Passing 'Black Cabs' can be hailed when their orange light is on, our you can pick one up from an official rank, including Lime Street Station, James Street Station, Adelphi Hotel, Hanover Street, Stanley Street, Sir Thomas Street and Chinatown.

PRIVATE HIRE TAXIS

ANFIELD TAXIS
0151 263 2222

DAVY LIVER LTD
0151 708 7080

DELTA
0151 922 7373

EXCEL RADIO CARS
0151 728 8888

MERSEY CABS
0151 207 2222

WIRRAL MERSEY CABS
0151 652 7777

EMERGENCY SERVICES

For the police, fire service, ambulance or coastguard, in an emergency dial 999.

MERSEYSIDE POLICE HQ
Canning Place
0151 709 6010

HEALTH

NHS DIRECT
0845 4647
www.nhsdirect.co.uk

NHS WALK-IN CENTRE
Great Charlotte Street L1

ROYAL LIVERPOOL HOSPITAL
Prescot Street L3
0151 706 2000

DENTAL HOSPITAL
Pembroke Place L3
0151 706 5050

MOSS CHEMISTS
68/70 London Road L3
0151 709 5271

CASHPOINTS

ALBERT DOCK CARDPOINT (CHARGES £1.84)
22 Edward Pavilion
Liverpool L3 4AD

LIVERPOOL ONE
NATWEST
49 South John Street
Liverpool L1 8BU

CAVERN WALKS
BARCLAYS BANK
46-50 Lord Street
Liverpool, L2 1TD

MATHEW STREET
HSBC
99-101 Lord Street
Liverpool L2 6PG

CLAYTON SQUARE
LLOYDS TSB
88-94 Church Street
Liverpool L1 3HD

DALE STREET
YORKSHIRE BANK
2 Moorfields
Liverpool L2 2BS

HOPE STREET
HSBC
Myrtle Street
Liverpool L1 9BP

THE METROPOLITAN CATHEDRAL
LLOYDS TSB
124 Mount Pleasant
Liverpool L3 5SR

BOLD STREET
HALIFAX PLC
30 Bold Street
Liverpool L1 4LF

POST OFFICES

1-3 South John Street
Liverpool L1 8BN

35-37 Leece Street
Liverpool L1 2TR
India Building, Water Street
Liverpool L2 0RR

PASSPORT OFFICE

LIVERPOOL REGIONAL PASSPORT OFFICE
101 Old Hall Street
Liverpool L3 9BD
0300 222 0000

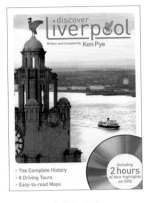

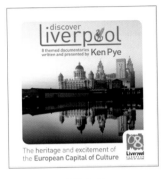

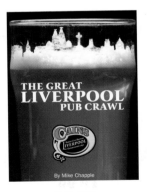

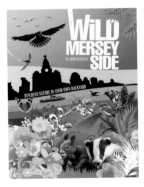

WWW.MERSEYSHOP.COM

£3.99
Liverpool Life

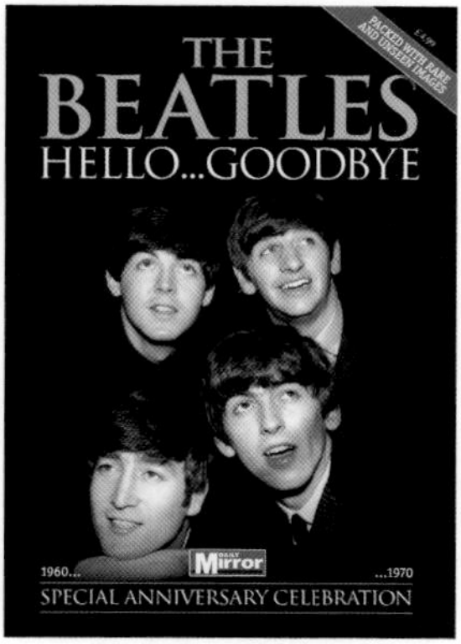

£4.99
The Beatles
Hello...Goodbye

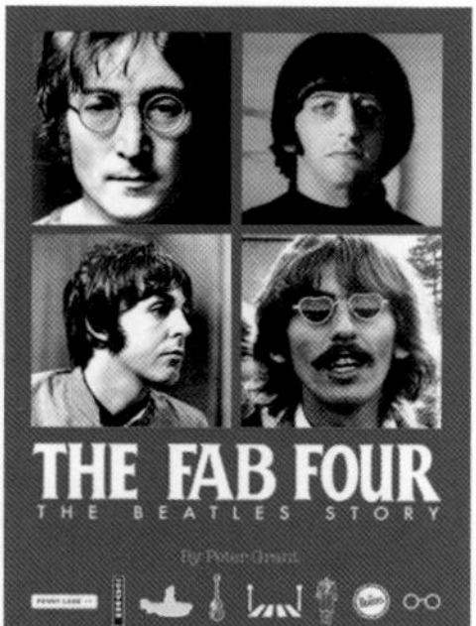

£3.99
The Fab Four

£8.99
The McCartneys:
In The Town Where
They Were Born

For current special offers and much more call 0845 143 0001

SOUTHPORT

A | B | LIVERPOOL FC
EVERTON FC

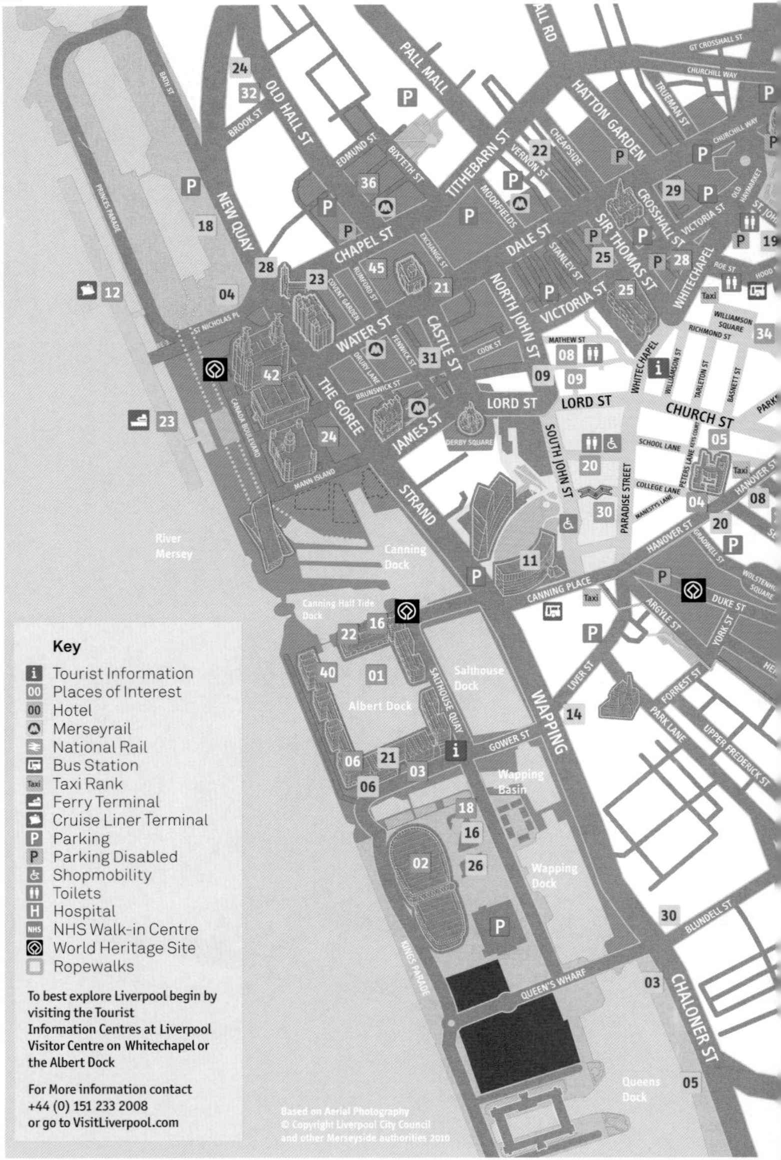

SCALE: 400M/3 MINUTES WALK

LIVERPOOL AIRPORT/SPEKE H
OTTERSPOOL PROMENADE

Key to Hotels and Tourist attractions in Liverpool city centre

Hotels

01 Aachen Hotel
02 Britannia Adelphi
03 Campanile
04 Crowne Plaza
05 Dolby
06 Express by Holiday Inn
07 Feathers
08 Hanover Hotel
09 Hard Days Night Hotel
10 Hatter's Hostel
11 Hilton Liverpool
12 Holiday Inn, City Centre
13 Hope Street Hotel
14 Ibis/Formule 1
15 International Inn
16 Jurys Inn
17 Lord Nelson Hotel
18 Malmaison
19 Marriott
20 Novotel
21 Premier Inn, Albert Dock
22 Premier Inn, City Centre
23 Racquet Club
24 Radisson Blu
25 Sir Thomas Hotel
26 Staybridge Suites
27 The Liner
28 Thistle (Atlantic Tower)
29 Travelodge
30 Youth Hostel
31 62 Castle Street

Tourist Attractions

01 Albert Dock
02 Arena and Convention Centre Liverpool
03 Beatles Story
04 Bluecoat Display Centre/Gifts
05 Bluecoat
06 Bugworld Experience
07 Cain's Brewery Tours
08 Cavern Club
09 Cavern Walks
10 Central Library
11 Clayton Square Shopping Centre
12 Cruise Liner Terminal
13 Empire Theatre
14 Everyman Theatre
15 FACT
16 International Slavery Museum
17 LIPA
18 Liverpool Big Wheel
19 Liverpool Cathedral
20 Liverpool ONE Shopping
21 Liverpool Town Hall
22 Maritime Museum
23 Mersey Ferries
24 Mersey Tunnel Tours
25 Metquarter
26 Metropolitan Cathedral
27 Mr Hardman's Photographic Studio
28 National Conservation Centre
29 NOVAS Contemporary Urban Centre
30 Odeon Cinema
31 Open Eye Gallery
32 Passport Office
33 Philharmonic Hall
34 Playhouse Theatre
35 Princes Road Synagogue
36 Register Office
37 Royal Court Theatre
38 St. George's Hall
39 St. John's Shopping Centre
40 Tate Liverpool
41 Unity Theatre
42 Underwater Street
43 Victoria Gallery & Museum
44 Walker Art Gallery
45 Western Approaches
46 World Museum Liverpool

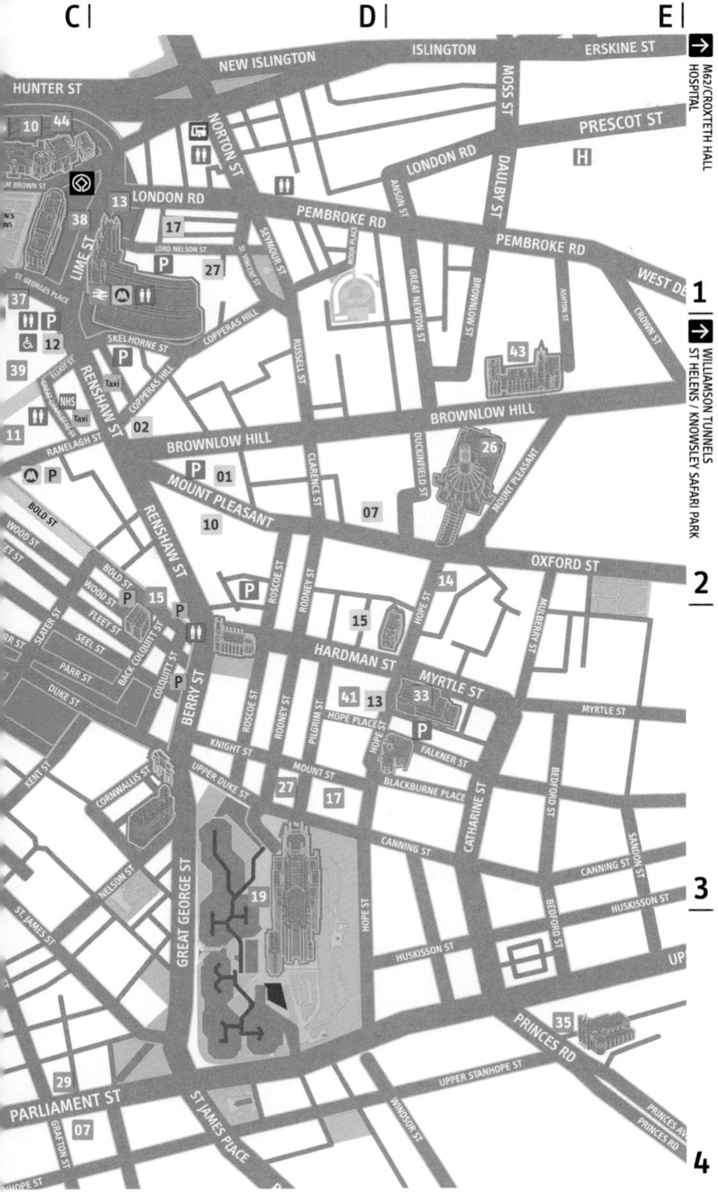
C
D
E
1
2
3
4
M62/CROXTETH HALL
HOSPITAL
WILLIAMSON TUNNELS
ST HELENS / KNOWSLEY SAFARI PARK
NEW ISLINGTON
ISLINGTON
ERSKINE ST
HUNTER ST
MOSS ST
PRESCOT ST
NORTON ST
LONDON RD
DAULBY ST
ANSON ST
PEMBROKE RD
LORD NELSON ST
ST. VINCENT ST
SEYMOUR ST
MOOR PLACE
GREAT NEWTON ST
BROWNLOW ST
ASHTON ST
WEST DE
CROWN ST
LIME ST
ST. GEORGES PLACE
SKELHORNE ST
COPPERAS HILL
RUSSELL ST
ELLIOT ST
RENSHAW ST
Taxi
NHS
GREAT CHARLOTTE ST
RANELAGH ST
BROWNLOW HILL
DUCKINFIELD ST
MOUNT PLEASANT
CLARENCE ST
BOLD ST
WOOD ST
OXFORD ST
ROSCOE ST
RODNEY ST
HOPE ST
MULBERRY ST
FLEET ST
SLATER ST
SEEL ST
BACK COLQUITT ST
PARR ST
COLQUITT ST
DUKE ST
HARDMAN ST
MYRTLE ST
BERRY ST
PILGRIM ST
HOPE PLACE
KNIGHT ST
FALKNER ST
MOUNT ST
UPPER DUKE ST
BLACKBURNE PLACE
CATHARINE ST
BEDFORD ST
KENT ST
CORNWALLIS ST
CANNING ST
SANDON ST
NELSON ST
HUSKISSON ST
ST. JAMES ST
GREAT GEORGE ST
UP
PRINCES RD
UPPER STANHOPE ST
PARLIAMENT ST
ST JAMES PLACE
WINDSOR ST
GRAFTON ST
PRINCES AV
HOPE ST
10
44
13
38
17
27
37
12
39
11
02
01
07
43
26
14
15
41
33
19
35
29